MACBETH

Edited by

(J.)H. WALTER

M.A., PH.D.

Formerly Headmaster
Minchenden School, Southgate
Fellow of University College
London

HEINEMANN EDUCATIONAL BOOKS

Heinemann Educational Books Ltd, Halley Court,
Jordan Hill, Oxford OX2 8EJ

OXFORD LONDON EDINBURGH
MELBOURNE SYDNEY AUCKLAND
IBADAN NAIROBI GABORONE HARARE
KINGSTON PORTSMOUTH NH (USA)
SINGAPORE MADRID

ISBN 0 435 19004 0

Reprinted 1963, 1965, 1967, 1968, 1969,
1972, 1973, 1975, 1976, 1977, 1978,
1981, 1982, 1985, 1986, 1987, 1988, 1989

Printed and bound in Great Britain by
Richard Clay Ltd, Bungay, Suffolk

CONTENTS

PREFACE

THE aim of this edition is to encourage pupils to study the play as a play, to see it not so much as a novel or a historical narrative, but as a pattern of speech and movement creating an artistic whole. While it has been generally accepted that this approach stimulates and enlivens classroom work, it has more recently become clear that it is a most fruitful way of preparing for examinations. The recent reports issued by the Cambridge Local Examinations Syndicate call attention to this aspect in the work of both Ordinary Level and Advanced Level candidates. The following comments are taken from the Advanced Level report:

'It will be seen that the best candidates are often those who show themselves conscious of the play as a made thing—usually, but by no means, always, as a thing made for the theatre' (p.5). Again, 'And perhaps the most misunderstood aspect of Shakespeare is the part played by theatrical convention . . .' (p. 6).

The interleaved notes, therefore, contain, in addition to a gloss, interpretations of character, dialogue and imagery, considered particularly from the point of view of a play. There are some suggestions for acting, for the most part simple pointers to avoid rigidity of interpretation and drawn up with an apron stage in mind. Some questions are interposed to provide topics for discussion or to assist in discrimination.

It is suggested that the play should be read through rapidly with as little comment as possible. On a second reading the notes should be used in detail, and appropriate sections of the Introduction might be read at the teacher's discretion.

It is hoped that this edition will enable the teacher to take his class more deeply into the play than the usual meagre allowance of time permits him to do; it is not an attempt to usurp his functions.

The play was not published before the First Folio Edition, 1623, and I have received much help from J. Dover Wilson's Facsimile Edition of this. I am also indebted to the modern editions of C. J. Sisson, J. Dover Wilson, G. L. Kittredge, K. Muir, and occasionally to the well-known

Preface

older editions. The text is complete. Stage directions follow in the main those of the Folio which was probably printed from the play-house prompt-copy. The locations of scenes added by previous editors have been placed in the notes.

Biblical quotations are from the *Bishops' Bible*, with the spelling modernized. References to Shakespeare's plays not yet published in this series are to the Tudor Edition (ed. P. Alexander), 1951.

Little reference has been made to textual difficulties and inconsistencies, and to the various theories that have been put forward to account for them. It seemed to me better to regard the play as a unity. The only divergence from this is in connexion with the Hecate scenes, and some views on these scenes are given in Appendix III. So much has been written about *Macbeth* that it is extremely difficult to acknowledge anything like all the debts that have been incurred.

I am aware that I have very gratefully drawn on the following studies: A. C. Bradley, *Shakespearian Tragedy*; R. T. Davies, *Four Centuries of Witch Beliefs*; G. R. Elliott, *Dramatic Providence in 'Macbeth'*; G. W. Knight, *The Imperial Theme*; K. A. Muir, *Shakespeare's Sources*; M. Murray, *The Witch Cult in Western Europe*; H. N. Paul, *The Royal Play of Macbeth*; W. Rosen, *Shakespeare and the Craft of Tragedy*; C. J. Sisson, *New Readings in Shakespeare*; B. Stirling, *Unity in Shakespearian Tragedy*; D. A. Traversi, *Approach to Shakespeare*; R. Walker, *The Time is Free*; L. Winstanley, *'Macbeth'*, *'King Lear'*, *and Contemporary History;* H. M. Hulme, *Explorations in Shakespeare's Language;* A. S. Venezky, *Pageantry on the Shakespearean Stage*.

Similarly I am indebted to articles in periodicals by W. A. Armstrong, W. Babcock, W. B. Bache, M. D. Burrell, L. A. Cormichan, H. N. Hulme, J. Jack, P. Kocher, A. E. Parsons, I. Ribner and E. Schanzer.

J.H.W.

INTRODUCTION

I

FIRST PERFORMANCES

On 17th July, 1606, King Christian IV of Denmark arrived on a brief visit to his sister Queen Anne. Hastily arranged pageantry greeted his royal entry into the city of London, he and James indulged in hunting at Greenwich, and drunken junketings at Theobalds, Cecil's home in Essex, but the day of distinction for him was 7th August. On that afternoon he was installed as a Knight of the Garter in St. George's Chapel, Windsor, in the presence of members of the Order in their scarlet and purple robes bearing the garter and the cross of St. George, 'signs of nobleness, like stars, . . . on all deservers'. In the evening the two kings were back at Hampton Court where they attended a play presented by James' royal players, the King's Men, Shakespeare's Company. The play was very probably *Macbeth*. It would be pleasant to imagine that the performance was so successful that it occasioned that lost 'amicable Letter', once reported to be in the possession of Sir William Davenant, Shakespeare's reputed godson, which 'King James the First, was pleas'd with his own Hand to write . . . to Mr. *Shakespeare*'.

The play may have been produced at about the same time at the Globe, though the first report of a performance there was recorded in 1611 by Dr. Simon Forman. Because his account of the play differs in some respects from the *Macbeth* we have, and because of some inconsistencies in the text, many critics have argued that alterations and cuts must have been made to the play in its original form. The purpose of these alterations is variously supposed to have been to shorten the play for a Court performance (James disliked long plays), to introduce topical matter following the execution of Garnet (see note to II. iii, 7) and the

3

visit of King Christian, and, at a later date, to introduce singing and dancing. The trend of opinion now seems to be that little has been cut from the play, and that that has been done without disturbing the impression of unity the play gives, that the Hecate scenes were added by another person (see Appendix III), not however the dramatist Middleton as had been generally assumed.

II

CRITICAL STATEMENTS

The content and presentation of *Macbeth* must have been satisfying to King James. It included many matters of known interest to him: demonology, the divine nature of kings, his legendary pedigree, the gift of touching for the evil, and it derided the equivocation of Garnet when charged with complicity in the Gunpowder Plot against his life. Its show of eight kings and Banquo complimented him by shaping the popular Nine Worthies' Pageant to include his ancestors. Yet it is not a mere charade to flatter him, it is finely integrated into a profound representation of evil unloosed, and this was a matter which James had elaborated in his *Fruitful Meditation*. For us first impressions are likely to be its frightening speed, its pitiless savagery, its evil energy, its see-saw of paradox and antithesis in word and act, its wry irony, and the 'fiery cohesion' of images erupting from Shakespeare's 'forgetive' mind. We may even be tempted to affix a quick moral label like 'crime does not pay' or 'good triumphs in the end'.

Much criticism can in fact be reduced, perhaps unfairly, to such labels—a study in fear; a nocturne of despair; the epilogue of the Histories (plays); conflict between reason and passion; a study of immoral man in a moral universe; Shakespeare's most profound and mature vision of evil; the greatest morality play; most sensible treatise on demonology; its essential structure is to be sought in its poetry; it is best interpreted through its themes and imagery, not through 'character'; a socio-political allegory. This and

4

similar writing about *Macbeth* may attempt to measure its qualities alongside prescribed patterns of tragedy derived particularly from medieval and renaissance theories, or to devise epigraphs mentioned above such as a 'tragedy of ambition' or a 'statement of evil', as comprehending the totality of the play. Still other writing directs attention to features in it that are common to Shakespeare's tragedies—waste, pride, or a fatal flaw in the character of the central figure. Valuable though all these are in enlarging and deepening one's impression of the play, it is important to realize that to analyse, compare and derive it in this way is to present only broken lights of the whole. Ideally the play should be experienced as a total movement in proper order yet the experience we take to the play is insufficient by itself; some parts of the play, indeed even its wholeness, may be meaningless unless we have some knowledge of Jacobean events and opinions. Even here there is no fixed Jacobean world picture; constant debunkings, rehabilitations and reappraisals change the composition and colouring from one decade to another. We can make only a tentative approach.

III

THE JACOBEAN UNIVERSE

Macbeth's choice of evil brings disorder and misery to society, disturbs the heavens and offers a threat to the frame of the universe. To appreciate the universal implications of his action and the cosmic images that express its reverberations, it is necessary to know some of the presuppositions of the period.

The whole of the universe was regarded as divinely ordered into degrees, all parts of creation had their positions fixed and their qualities determined and made purposive, all were intricately linked in the great chain of being. The stability or concord of the universe, or macrocosm, was maintained by the balancing of opposites (for everything had its opposite), and by the will of things to maintain their individual purposes. There was also a system of correspondences between the macrocosm, the micro-cosm (man), and the kingdom, so that events in the one involved analogous events in the others. When in *Julius Cæsar* Brutus out in the storm confesses his uncertainties about murdering Cæsar he makes a natural comparison: 'the state of man, Like to a little kingdom, suffers then The nature of an insurrection' (II. i, 67–9). The correspondence between the sun in the heavens and a king on earth underlies Ross's remark on the darkness of the morning after Duncan's murder:

> by th' clock 'tis day,
> And yet dark night strangles the travelling lamp . . .
> . . . darkness does the face of the earth entomb,
> When living light should kiss it?

Any unnatural or inverted action therefore, such as that by Duncan's horses, was a violent breach of the divine order of things. Kings were God's regents to be given complete obedience, rebellion therefore was a crime against God. Satan, the rebel against God, was the instigator of all subsequent rebellions against the divine order; witches and evil spirits were his agents and were employed by him in fomenting rebellion.

IV

WITCHCRAFT AND POSSESSION

To appreciate the violent, unreasoning thoughts and feelings the Weird Sisters probably aroused in Jacobean audiences, it is necessary to know something of the terrifying witch mania that sprang up in Elizabeth's reign, lessened slightly its fury as rational opinions spread during the latter part of the reign of James I, but lingered on into the eighteenth century. Treatises by well-known continental scholars such as Bodin, Remi, Daneau, Delrio were published, together with a number of English treatises derived largely from them, affirming belief in witchcraft and the neces-sity for exterminating all witches, and containing horrifying accounts of brutal and gruesome witch trials in which not a few of the accused and their judges appear to have eaten freely of the 'insane root that takes the reason prisoner'. There was also a flood of popular pamphlets describing notable witch trials in England and Scotland. The influence of the former was particularly strong on the better-read sections of society because of the rationalized form in which it was presented; the popular accounts fomented the more primitive superstitions among the less learned.

Parliament drafted an Act, which was not made law until 1563, making murder by witchcraft punishable by death, thus accepting that witches existed and that they had magical powers. A similar act declaring that anyone found guilty of practising witchcraft of any kind should be executed was made law in 1604. Both acts were intended to protect the monarch from the spells of witchcraft practised, it was alleged, by Roman Catholics, and particularly as it was held on scriptural authority that rebellion and witchcraft went hand in hand.

Many of the persons accused of witchcraft were poor, old women, and their victims were also humble, but no class was exempt. The Earl of Derby was thought to have been killed by witchcraft in 1594; Francis Stewart, Earl of Bothwell, was accused of conjuring and witchcraft against James, and Dr. Fian and the witches of Berwick were found guilty of trying to destroy James and Anne his bride by raising storms at sea, during their voyage from Denmark to Scotland in 1590. It has been estimated that some eight thousand witches were burned in Scotland in the forty years before James came to the throne of England; on the continent the numbers burnt may have reached hundreds of thousands; in England, no complete records are available, but the numbers must have been greater than in Scotland.

James, his interest stimulated by the trials of the Berwick witches at which he was present, wrote a treatise on witchcraft, *Demonology*, 1597, and he maintained his interest by investigating in person the cases of supposed witchcraft reported to him. He considered that he was persecuted by the forces of evil because he was destined to restore the empire of King Arthur.

It is immaterial whether Shakespeare drew on Scot's *Discovery of Witchcraft*, 1584, or James' *Demonology*, 1597—there are signs that he consulted both—or any of the other numerous works. The powers and qualities attributed to the Weird Sisters are part of the commonplaces of witch-lore. In brief they had power to raise storms and fog, and to hold back day or bring on night. They could strike men or women with sterility, kill animals, cause their enemies to waste away, bring fearful nightmares, and induce demoniacal possession of any person. They could move invisibly through the air and sail the seas on a sieve; they had powers of prophecy and of raising evil spirits. To each one Satan gave a familiar spirit in the form of a beast, bird or reptile which was suckled by the witch. A woman (or man) could only become a witch by her own freely expressed wish. Satan himself, or someone who represented Satan, sucked from such an applicant drops of blood, to seal her as his. The spot on her body from which the blood was drawn remained a permanent red mark, the Devil's mark of the witch-finders. Groups (covens) of witches held meetings (sabbats) which the Devil, or particularly in Scotland Diana (Hecate), might attend, usually to give instructions or to demonstrate some illusion to deceive mortals, or by a hideous brew to raise spirits. Witches were urged to seek vengeance on their enemies just before the meetings ended with a round dance.

V

WITCHCRAFT, POSSESSION, AND THE PLAY

The Weird Sisters have defied precise definition. They have been called 'old hags' and 'elemental forces'; in fact opinion about them has classified them in varying degrees from water-nymphs to norns. It is usual to regard them as part of an external evil force, ever in ambush, that assaults Macbeth when pride of success has made him vulnerable. They stir his secret desires into conscious formulation and provide him with access to evil. This detached, modern view is remote from the intense involvement of Jacobeans with the concreteness of evil, and it ignores, or interprets differently, the subtle evil and far-reaching transformations in Macbeth and Lady Macbeth.

Jacobeans would have had no hesitation in recognizing in Macbeth's words and actions implications of demoniac possession. Shakespeare is not clinically explicit in the matter, but there are significant words and some ambiguities of speech and action. Characteristics common to the various forms of possession were a change or distortion of face, a change of voice, change in character, a kind of trance or raptness in one form of which, though aware of his state the victim is compelled to speak and act against his will, and a numbness of senses. He sometimes forgets what took place in the immediately preceding state of mind, and he is unable to pray.

Macbeth's first meeting with the witches causes him to start and become 'rapt' (I. iii, 57, 142); he seeks more knowledge, but his mind and will are at variance, and later he excuses his raptness to his companions, 'my dull brain was wrought with things forgotten.' On three occasions Lady Macbeth calls attention to his changed features (I. v, 60–1; III. ii, 27; III. iv, 67). After the murder of Duncan he is unable to say 'Amen' to the prayer he overheard (II. ii, 29–33). There are further signs of raptness and inner compulsion in the dagger-scene (II. i, 33–64). In III. iv, the appearance of Banquo's ghost calls forth from Macbeth his damning utterances, his 'strange infirmity', regardless of his guests. Later, he comments on his insensibility to fear (V. v, 9–15), and his reception of the news of his wife's death shows a remote indifference (V. v, 17–18).

In this way Macbeth's sharply divided personality which commentators have noted, had its justification in contemporary demonology. In the trance-like state of possession the evil spirit speaks through Macbeth, but in his normal state he can weigh the moral issues of the murder, and has sufficient conscience afterwards to realize some of its consequences; unable to resist the compulsion of evil he commits the murder, yet is clearly aware of his deadly treachery.

In a similar way the evil corruption spreads in Lady Macbeth, though the signs are more those of a witch as such than of a demoniac. Women, it was believed, were more prone to witchcraft than men. Lady Macbeth speedily and freely invokes the evil spirits to possess her; her words, 'Come to my woman's breasts and take my milk for gall' recall the suckling by witches of their familiar spirits. Moreover, it was also believed that familiar spirits so sucking spread infection throughout the witch's body. Water would not touch a witch because she had renounced the water of baptism, so that Lady Macbeth's hand washing during her sleep-walking has this dire aspect. More sinister still is the 'damned spot'. It can be regarded as a mere guilt sign, the product of an over-wrought mind, but the audience would surely have assumed that it was the Devil's mark on one who had given her soul to the Devil and was therefore a witch herself. The Doctor's verdict after witnessing the sleep-walking, 'More needs she the divine than the physician,' may be taken quite simply to mean that Lady Macbeth should seek to confess her sins, but it could more effectively be taken to mean that she needs a priest to exorcise the spirit that has possessed her and caused her trance and confession. Her death is obscure—

> Who as 'tis thought, by self and violent hands
> Took off her life (V. ix, 36–7),

in fact, it is characteristic of many accused of witchcraft who when in prison managed to commit suicide, or who died strangely by devilish aid.

VI

MACBETH

It is sometimes said that Macbeth represents Adam sinning or Satan rebelling, that the utter disintegration and corruption of his being is a mirror of primal conceptions. Such views enlarge his significance outside his own narrow 'bank and shoal of time' and place; not only is he involved with all mankind, but his actions distort the great chain of being that is the universe. Within his own soul his chain of murders diminishes him until shrunken in understanding, isolated from love, he reaches the hell of his own creation, 'I am myself alone'. So much of the play is given through the experience of Macbeth, the man, as distinct from the figure or symbol that universalizes him, or even relates him to events in Shakespeare's England, that his human-kindness is a basic consideration.

The enigmatic words of the Witches, sworn to vengeance, bode ill towards Macbeth before he appears. Yet the description of his feats in battle in epic terms shows his greatness as a general, his courage, hardihood and success, and above all he is the preserver of his king and country from rebellion and foreign invasion. His position in society is secure, he is loved and respected by all, honoured and rewarded above others by his sovereign to whom he gives allegiance. This is his rightful position under the divinely appointed king. The prophecy of the Witches, enlarging his pride in his success, arouses in his imagination evil possibilities, or the recognition of an evil temptation, or even the freezing fear of demoniac possession. He rejects the evil thought, but the conflict in his mind has begun.

Macbeth too possesses amiable qualities of gentle kindness, justness, obedience to God, truthfulness, though Lady Macbeth, considers these as impediments to her plan. Moreover his soliloquy at supper time moves from practical considerations and self-interest through the honourable observance of social obligations, to a sensitive appreciation of Duncan's virtues and the universal compassion his death would cause. So far an audience may be involved with Macbeth; his success, virtues and human decency are common ground.

This soliloquy does other things. By praising and elevating Duncan, not hitherto described, the murder is put into perspective. At the same time the echo of Christ's words to Judas, and the parallel with the Last Supper exposes the thread of evil in Macbeth, even though he finds no cause for murdering Duncan but 'vaulting ambition' that defeats itself; his succumbing to his wife's overwhelming assault on his courage is therefore to be expected. Shakespeare departing significantly from Holinshed's version deprives Macbeth of any justifiable motive for murdering Duncan.

Macbeth moves to the murder trance-like as if under some compulsive force, aware of the nature of the deed, yet unable to prevent himself doing it. Once done, Macbeth awakes to the spiritual consequences to himself, which neither he nor his wife had considered. He cannot pray, he has 'murdered sleep'. His guilt is universal, he has destroyed the divine order, the 'breach in nature', and let in chaos, 'ruin's wasteful entrance', by his sacrilegious destruction of the 'Lord's anointed temple'. Whether his lament over Duncan is hypocritical and ironical, or whether he really loved Duncan and spoke the truth is debatable. His savage slaughter of the grooms may curiously be an attempt to express in action this love, or again a wild silencing of their mouths.

His increasing corruption spreads outwardly in the state and within himself. He moves apart from his wife to plan the murder of Banquo with a callousness that contrasts with his former sensitiveness. He jeers at the christian doctrine of loving one's enemies. His fearful invocation to Night to break the bond of nature, the fixed order of the universe, is a presumptuous, satanic challenge, a wish for universal chaos that occurred earlier to him (III. ii, 16) and remains with him to the end (V. v, 49–50).

At his banquet the inversion of order and the unnaturalness he has loosed overthrows him, the dead Banquo rises and occupies Macbeth's seat. The emblematic nature of this is clear, Banquo's spirit will ultimately supplant Macbeth, and Macbeth is unable to join an ordered society, in fact he is cut off from it and can only bring an 'admired disorder'. He learns that he is vulnerable, and in his fear and horror boasts defiantly. In desperation he visits the Weird Sisters, determined to seek knowledge if not security even at the cost of destroying all nature's germens and the concord of creation. Herod-like he kills Macduff's children, his third offence against specific christian teaching. There is a hint of madness (V. ii, 13), of shrinkage of authority and a recognition of the loss of human society—'love, honour, troops of friends'. His feelings deaden, and the life he bitterly describes as futile, 'signifying nothing' is the frustration of desire, opportunity and hope.

At last he realizes the 'equivocation of the fiend', that has stripped him of the qualities that raise man above the beasts, and as a beast he dies. Unlike the first Cawdor who 'set forth a deep repentance', Macbeth invokes damnation on himself and dies in the deepest of all sins that of impenitence.

VII

LADY MACBETH

Lady Macbeth is everywhere practical and expedient. Her appeal to the 'spirits that tend on mortal thoughts' is conceived in material terms. Her single-minded purpose is the murder of Duncan to achieve 'sovereign sway'. Though it has been stated that she loves her husband, there is no direct evidence of it, unless her exclamation, 'My husband!' (II. ii, 14) be so interpreted. She effectively extinguishes all scruples, and with machiavellian amorality resolutely and passionately goads Macbeth to commit the murder. She is indeed 'possessed' by evil spirits although at times there are touches of normality. Her comment on Duncan 'Had he not resembled My father as he slept, I had done 't' may be one of the 'compunctious visitings of nature' that came unawares, as the reality of murder pressed on her. After the murder does her famous 'A little water clears us of this deed' show inability to grasp what has happened to Macbeth, or is it a determination to keep things at a superficial, material level—'These deeds must not be thought After these ways'? Is her faint real or a device to divert attention from her husband? There is some ambiguity in her actions, for in III. ii she is clearly aware of the spiritual consequences of the crime:

> Nought's had, all's spent,
> Where our desire is got without content.

She is unable to break down Macbeth's increasing isolation, the two are now irreconcilably apart. During the banquet scene she makes a tremendous effort to control Macbeth's terror. This time the accusation of cowardice cannot drive away his fears, and she has no resources of spirit—she seems unaware of any moral order—with which to comfort him. Sleep denies her any healing, unnatural somnambulism with re-tracing of past conversations and thoughts about the crimes shows a mind in process of disintegration to the ultimate despair of suicide. Is she the fiend-like Queen who tries vainly to erase the Devil's mark from her hand, is she an incomplete figure, a necessary spring to Macbeth's fall, or is she in fact one aspect of Macbeth himself? Whatever answer we make, she greatly stirs our terror and pity.

VIII

SOME INTERPRETATIONS

The three following interpretations of parts of the play are put forward for consideration. A form of construction which appears to have escaped notice arises from the morality aspect of the play. In morality tradition virtues and vices have their 'houses', the centres of virtuous or vicious activity. The pattern is clearly shown in Spenser's *Faerie Queene* where the knight-errant journeys to the 'house' of the virtue he represents for refreshment, instruction, and aid after suffering disaster, or where Duessa journeys for help to hell from the House of Pride. In *Macbeth* Macduff and Malcolm have taken a journey to Edward's court where in a kind of House of Divine Kingship the ideal of kingship is debated, and where they see a sanctified king in action. In balanced contrast Macbeth in desperate fear journeys to the 'pit of Acheron', the House of Hell, to seek help and encouragement. Both sides are fortified by their visits and prepare for the final encounter.

It has been alleged that IV. iii has no dramatic value: it is a mere treatise on ideal kingship, together with a blatant piece of flattery of James I over the royal 'touch', the whole made less boring by the announcement of the slaughter of Macduff's family. It is much more than that. Malcolm's fencing with Macduff is not without tension, for if Macduff is prepared to urge Malcolm to return, whatever vices he claims to have, then he is indeed an agent from Macbeth. At the same time the vices he names are an indictment of Macbeth, and the virtues he disclaims build up the ideal of kingship to which we assume he subscribes, and which is further elaborated by the account of Edward's healing touch and the sundry blessings that hang about his throne. The importance of this latter in the morality construction has been mentioned above. From another point of view the healing in this scene balances the murder of sleep, the healing principle, by Macbeth; and the sanctity of Edward's court balances the hell that is Macbeth's castle where no healing is possible either for Lady Macbeth or for the realm. Although events begin to turn against Macbeth in the banqueting scene, so far we have viewed events mainly through his agitated mind. Now the focus is

moved so that we see him from outside in a complete condemnation of his rule.

The Porter's scene is not intrusive, ribald vulgarity to keep the
groundlings amused, it develops important themes prevalent
elsewhere in the play, it is a brilliant sardonic chorus comment
on the dramatic situation. Its comedy does not bring relief, its
laughter vibrates the nerves almost to breaking. Lady Macbeth
and Macbeth have created their own state of hell by their invocations and the murder, the Porter in his fuddled, ironic performance as hell-porter drives home the point to the audience.
Henceforth Macbeth has committed himself to hell, the frustration of all desires and opportunities, and the alone-ness which
keeps him outside the understanding of his wife. The implied
reference to Garnet, 'hanged without equivocation' in 1606,
suddenly brings Macbeth's crime vividly forward as a contemporary issue and a perennial evil. So too does the reference to the
unnaturalness of the farmer, an alias of Garnet, who commits
suicide for fear of an abundant harvest. Equivocation, unnaturalness and unfruitfulness are major themes of the play.

The exposition of the effect of drink on lechery, like much else
in the play is antithetical in its parts; it is a fiendishly mocking
variation on Lady Macbeth's comment 'That which hath made
them drunk hath made me bold; What hath quenched them hath
given me fire.' But in the prominence it gives to the frustration
of desire it mirrors another aspect of hell. The association of lust
with murder in a context of rebellion need not occasion surprise.
The *Homily Against . . . Rebellion* denounces rebellion as the
'whole puddle and sink of all sins against God and man'. Shakespeare elsewhere links the two in *Titus Andronicus*, V. ii, the *Rape
of Lucrece*, l. 168, *Macbeth* itself (II. i, 52–6) and *Pericles*, I. i, 137–9:

> One sin I know another doth provoke:
> Murder's as near to lust as flame to smoke.
> Poison and treason are the hands of sin.

IX

THEMES

The Weird Sisters herald an attack on Macbeth by the forces of evil employing deceit, illusion and equivocation. Involved with his ruin is the disruption of the divine unity and harmony of individual man, living creatures, the family, society, the age and the heavens. Consequently the simple movement of the play is varied, enlarged and deepened by themes, motifs, images, overtones and echoes making manifest the totality of the assault and the growth of resistance to it. Some are sustained throughout the play, others describing an emotion or thought recur tinged with irony, and others hint at subtle links of feeling. Momentarily they may reflect an allegorical way of thinking, become symbols of matters of life and death, or flash out literary or proverbial associations and enlightenings.

Of the evil-born themes, false appearance is integral to the play. The Sisters announce it with 'Fair is foul, and foul is fair', and Macbeth's first echoing words, 'So foul and fair a day I have not seen', link his destiny immediately with their evil. Duncan, deceived by the false appearance that concealed Cawdor's treachery, deplores such deceit in the form of a proverb that serves as an ironical introit for the immediate entry of Macbeth, the new and already tainted Cawdor:

'There's no art
To find the mind's construction in the face (I. iv, 11–12)

In (I. vii, 82) 'False face must hide what the false heart doth know', and (III. ii, 34–5) 'And make our faces vizards to our hearts, Disguising what they are'. Macbeth declares the false appearance he assumes to hide his intentions from his victim and his friends. Lady Macbeth's assertion of false appearance, 'The sleeping and the dead Are but as pictures' (II. ii, 53-4), is a specious attempt to restore Macbeth's courage. In a similar way the prophecies of the apparitions (IV. i, 71-94) give to Macbeth the false appearance of security which 'is mortals' chiefest enemy'. Malcolm's resolute 'Though all things foul would wear the brows of grace, Yet grace must still look so' (IV. iii, 23-4) marks a kind of turning point. Hitherto false appearance has given Macbeth success, now by a kind of inversion characteristic of the play it aids the virtuous by the branches of Birnam Wood to destroy him.

Interplaying and merging with the theme of false appearance is the allied theme of equivocation. It is implicit in the plotting of Macbeth and Lady Macbeth, and it bursts out ironically from Macbeth in his two emotionally-tensed speeches after the discovery of Duncan's murder where his surface lies reveal a deeper truth (II. iii, 84-9; 101-11). The Porter's scene which conjures up a hellish image of the play, accompanied by an apt commentary, defines the equivocator. It writhes the feelings with its jocular description of drink equivocating lechery, the same drink that drenched the grooms and emboldened Lady Macbeth, and so equivocated Duncan to death. Later, equivocation together with false appearance informs Macbeth's speeches and actions as his mind becomes more deeply corrupt. The equivocation of the two prophecies of Birnam Wood and 'none of woman born' entice Macbeth to his doom.

Night, darkness or gloom envelop Macbeth's castle and his moral sense; Night generates evil things, and is invoked to aid and conceal evil (I. iv, 50-2; v, 48-52; II. i, 49-56; III. ii, 46-53), and maintains an atmosphere of fear (II. i, 4-9; 56-60; II. iv, 5-10; III. ii, 17-22). Under this blanket of the dark proliferates the theme of disorder in the heavens and among creatures (II. iv, 1-20). Disorder spreads in society (III. iv, 40-119), in the family (IV. ii), and in men's minds (I. iii, 130-42; IV. ii, 18-22). Another theme, unnaturalness, accompanies disorder: the deformity of

evil (I. iii, 41–7), the broken bodies of living creatures that feed
evil (IV. i, 5–38), the inversion of natural processes (II. iv, 6–20),
Lady Macbeth's invocations (I. v, 38–48) and her illness (V. i,
71–2), and even Macduff's flight (IV. ii, 8–11). Unnatural too in
a fruitful universe are barrenness and sterility, the marks of evil:
the withered witches (I. iii, 40), the blasted heath (I. iii, 77), Lady
Macbeth's unsexing (I. v, 38–41), the threat to destroy Nature's
germens (IV. i, 58–60), Macbeth's barrenness (III. i, 61–4), and
his evil attempt to extirpate Banquo's race (III. iii) and Macduff's
family (IV. ii).

Another aspect of disorder is the murder of sleep, the healer
and restorer, by Macbeth, from whom it is then wrenched by
hideous dreams (III. ii, 21–2); and in Lady Macbeth it is distorted
into sleep-walking and the loss of its healing qualities. Disease
similarly is a theme of evil. It is within the witches' gift (I. iii, 2,
18–23), afflicts Lady Macbeth's mind (V. i; iii, 40), and describes the state of Scotland under Macbeth's rule (V. ii, 15, 27–30;
iii, 50–6).

In opposition to the themes and images sprung from evil there
are others that give shape to the establishment of harmony and
grace. There is emphasis on the divinity and grace of a king
(I. vii, 16–20; II. iii, 61–3, 87; III. i, 66; III. vi, 3, 10, 30; IV. iii,
108–11, 140–59). Images of fertility and growth often linked
with Duncan and Malcolm abound. Macbeth's castle in the presence of Duncan is seen as the martlet's 'procreant cradle'. Duncan
'plants' Macbeth and 'will labour' to make him 'full of growing'.
Banquo, embraced, promises the harvest from his growth to
Duncan (I. iv, 29–33). Malcolm echoes his father's word and
undertakes to 'plant' for the future (V. ix, 31). The royal powers
of healing are expressly described in IV. iii, 141–59, and the more
general theme is mentioned in II. ii, 36–9; IV. iii, 214–15; V. iii,
39–47; and the healing of a nation in V. ii, 27–30; iii, 50–4. The list
of kingly virtues, and of those qualities that conserve a state's
unity, peace and concord (IV. iii, 91–100) sum up the theme of

order. Indeed the words are weighted in that James I's love of peace was reflected in the pageant figure of Concord that greeted him and Christian, they were probably also known from the Litany— 'to give to all nations unity, peace and concord', and the prayer for the Church Militant— 'inspire continually the universal Church with the spirit of truth, unity and concord'. By Concord, as Spenser noted, God bound heaven and the world in 'inviolable bands', otherwise 'hell them quight'. The order of Duncan's court is implicit in his announcement of the succession, his bounty and the bond that links them all (I. iv, 35–43), and his assumption that they are bound in love (I. vi, 10–30). Even dogs are 'ordered' (III. i, 92–101). Other aspects of order occur in III. vi, 32–7; V. iii, 24–6; and in the final speech of Malcolm V. ix, 26–41, confirming that 'the time is free'.

Other recurring images some of which support the larger themes are concerned with the eye and what it sees (I. iv, 52–3; II. i, 33–49; II. ii, 51–9, etc.), clothing (I. vii, 36; V. ii, 20–2, etc.), a babe or child (I. vii, 21, 54–8; IV. i. 77–89; IV. ii).

Over a hundred references explicit and implicit to blood have been counted; even though few are killed on the stage the image sets the sinister and deadly tone of the play. Significance, too, may be attached to the frequent appearance of the word 'strange' with meanings ranging from peculiar to occult, to the eight references to heaven (heavenly) in IV. iii, and to the frequent allusions to time in various senses. These are by no means exhaustive.

X

BIBLICAL ALLUSIONS

There are a number of echoes of phrases and sentences from the Bible which, in view of the christian connotations of the play, reveal a rich significance when linked with their biblical contexts. There is also imagery suggestive of judgement, grace and sacrament.

The description of the miseries of Scotland under Macbeth,

horrors beyond anything suggested before (IV. iii, 4–8, 164–76) taken with the satanic nature of Macbeth (IV. iii, 55–7) have been regarded as prompted by the theme of *Revelation*, xx. 7–10, the temporary loosing of Satan on the world, aided by James I's interpretation of those four verses in his *Fruitful Meditation*. Elsewhere in the play imagery reminiscent of *Revelation* has been noted: 'angels, trumpet-tongued . . . cherubin' (I. vii, 19–22), 'great doom's image . . . graves rise up' (II. iii, 72–3). Although many parallels have been suggested for the 'multitudinous . . . green one red' (II. ii, 62–3), it may well owe something to *Revelation*, xvi. 3, 'the second angel shed out his vial [of the wrath of God] upon the sea, and it . . . the blood of a dead man, and every living thing died in the sea', as a punishment for those who bore the 'mark of the beast', and who had slain the saints. Macbeth's bitter complaint 'full of scorpions is my mind' (III. ii, 36) recalls the creatures with torment of a scorpion loosed out of hell under Apollyon to torment those 'men which have not the seal of God in their foreheads' but who still did not repent of 'their murders, and of their sorceries . . .' (*Revelation*, ix, 3–11, 21).

Macbeth's evil, treachery and devilish nature is underlined. From the first he is the 'man of blood', the 'bloody man' accursed in the *Psalms*, v. 6; lv. 23 and in 2 *Samuel*, xvi. 7. He sneers at the central teaching of the Sermon on the Mount, 'Are you so gospelled To pray for this good man' (III. i, 88–9) i.e. to 'pray for them which hurt you, and persecute you' (*St. Matthew*, v. 44), and urges revenge as do all Satan's followers. Macbeth's withdrawal from supper hints at his Judas' nature and the symbolism of the supper itself. His words 'If it were . . . quickly' (I. vii, 1–2) recall the situation in *St. John*, xiii. 27, 30: 'And after the sop, Satan entered into him. Then said Jesus unto him, That thou doest, do quickly' . . . 'as soon then as he had received the sop, he went immediately out: and it was night'.

His hands bloody from the shedding of innocent blood, or

with 'secret murders sticking' on them, are condemned *Proverbs*, vi. 17; *Isaiah*, lix. 3, but his own outcry after the murder may echo *Isaiah*, i. 15, 'And when ye spread forth your hands, I will hide mine eyes from you; yea, when ye make many prayers, I will not hear: your hands are full of blood'. Later Malcolm uses words of Macbeth that link him with Satan. 'When I shall tread upon the tyrant's head' (IV. iii, 45) with 'I will also put enmity between thee and her seed: it shall tread down thy head' (*Genesis*, iii. 14).

The sanctity of Duncan and the enormity of his murder is indicated not only at the supper, but also after his death by Macduff's cry 'sacrilegious murder hath broke ope The Lord's anointed temple' (II. iii, 61–2) which combines 'ye are the temple of the living God' (2 *Corinthians*, vi. 16) with 'I will not put forth my hand against my Lord; for he is the Lord's anointed' (1 *Samuel*, xxiv. 10), and *St. John*, ii. 21 where Christ 'spake of the temple of his body'. The phrases used by Macbeth 'Renown and grace is dead, The wine of life is drawn, and the mere lees Is left this vault to brag of' (II. iii, 87–9) it has been suggested may refer to *Psalms*, lxxv. 8, 'For in the hand of the Lord there is a cup, and the wine is red; it is full of mixture; and he poureth out of the same; but the dregs thereof, all the wicked of the earth shall wring them out, and drink them'. Yet the image is closer to the wine of the communion sacrament with its pledge of everlasting life, and this too may hint, as did the supper, at a Christlike king. Further references to the grace and holiness of Duncan and his wife, the 'most sainted King' and the Queen who 'Oftener upon her knees than on her feet, Died every day she lived' (IV. iii, 109–11) adapts a sentence of St. Paul, 'I die daily' (*I Corinthians*, xv. 31).

The hapless wife of Macduff laments with bitterness his defection with 'All is the fear, and nothing is the love' (IV. ii, 12), a sad echo of 'There is no fear in love, but perfect love casteth out fear . . . he that feareth is not perfect in love' (*I John*, iv. 18).

Her son's suggestion that he will live 'As birds do', drawn from *St. Matthew*, vi. 26, 'Behold the fowls of the air; for they sow not . . .' i.e. that he will not be anxious about material things, but will rely on God's care, intensifies almost unbearably the bitterness and pathos of their fate.

Macbeth's despair at the futility of existence, 'And all our yesterdays have lighted fools The way to dusty death. Out, out, brief candle! Life's but a walking shadow' (V. v, 22–4) is the more poignant from its association with *Job*, viii. 9, 'For we are but of yesterday, and are ignorant: for our days upon earth are but a shadow', and xviii. 6, 'The light shall be dark in his dwelling, and his candle shall be put out with him' particularly in its context. Job has lost hope—'It shall go down to the bars of Sheol, when once there is rest in the dust (xvii. 16)', and Bildad after the verses above goes on to describe the fate of the wicked men afflicted by terrors who 'shall have neither son nor son's son among his people' (xviii. 19).

By contrast Malcolm's final speech with its 'by the grace of Grace' recalls again the Christ-like theme, 'And of his [Christ's] fulness have all we received, and grace for grace' (*St. John*, i, 16).

XI

DEVICES OF STYLE

Elizabethan schooling provided training in rhetoric, that is the art of using words to persuade, to emphasize, and to display eloquence and wit. A most complex system of large numbers of figures of speech, devices of style and processes of thought had been formulated, and Shakespeare made extensive use of them. While for the most part it is enough to be aware that Shakespeare's apparent spontaneous ease in writing discloses a considerable knowledge of rhetoric, the particular use of a few devices in this play should be noted.

The themes of equivocation, disorder, false appearance and illusion, the enigmas and ambiguities, are caught up and reflected in the phrasing of the play to the intensifying and enriching of the total impression. Inversion of meaning, antitheses, paradox, oxymoron and the juxtaposition of opposites are liberally employed. They are the outward symptoms of the infection of evil springing from the witches or from Macbeth's corrupted mind. All who come into contact with the witches, and even those who are Macbeth's victims, or who talk of Macbeth's actions signal the presence and contradiction of evil with such devices.

In the first phase of the play, the crushing of the rebellion up to Duncan's arrival at Macbeth's castle, from the Witches' preludal 'lost and won', 'fair is foul' they are significantly spread. The Captain repeats the 'fair is foul' note, in the evil rebellion 'discomfort' ousts the expected 'comfort'. Duncan's 'What he hath lost, noble Macbeth hath won' offers one interpretation of the witches' riddling words which binds Macbeth to them, as do his first words, 'So foul and fair a day.' The contradictory nature of the witches is shown further in their 'lesser', 'greater'; 'not so happy', 'yet much happier', in Banquo's comment 'honest trifles, to betray's', and openly debated by Macbeth's speech on the antithesis 'Cannot be ill, cannot be good' leading to the annihilating paradox, 'nothing is But what is not'. Duncan too is involved in the reversals of values. The 'swiftest wing' is 'slow', his 'plenteous joys' express themselves in 'drops of sorrow', and the 'love' that follows him is his 'trouble'—it is indeed.

Later, the pressure of evil weighs on Banquo's mind: 'heavy summons', 'I would not sleep'; 'lose none', 'augment'. Verbal contradictions accompany the disorder and unnaturalness described by Ross and the Old Man, who sums up the situation: 'old robes', 'new'; 'good', 'bad'; 'friends', 'foes'. Lady Macduff is afflicted: 'wisdom', 'madness'; 'fear', 'love'; 'fathered', 'fatherless'; 'harm', 'laudable'; 'good', 'folly'.

The elaborate development of the idea of equivocation in the Porter's scene is expressed largely by means of contradictory phrases and antitheses. The massing of such constructions and figures gives considerable colour to the Porter's performance as the turnkey of hell.

Lady Macbeth, an associate in evil, describes her husband's virtues as if they were defects: 'wouldst not play false', 'wouldst wrongly win'; 'do', 'undone'; and in the self-contradiction of her deprived womanhood hell is to blanket out heaven, the 'future' replaces the 'ignorant present', and 'done double, Were poor and single business'. Her contempt for Macbeth's lingering goodness has expressive opposites: 'slept', 'wakes'; 'act', 'desire'; 'man', 'beast', and the drink that 'quenched' the grooms gave her 'fire'. Finally the ironic reversals of her earlier attitudes apparent in the sleep-walking scene are pointed by 'slumbery agitation'; 'sleep', 'watching'; 'done', 'undone'; 'eyes are open', 'their sense are shut', this last is an apt image of Lady Macbeth's limitations.

IV. iii is an astonishing tour de force, in it as a form of construction evil is opposed to grace in social settings placed squarely against each other. After Malcolm unspeaks his 'own detraction', his virtues are clearly depicted from the vices he previously admitted and the virtues he denied. The whole is completed by the grace, sanctity and blessings of Edward's court balanced against the miseries and ills of Scotland.

Macbeth's approach to Duncan's chamber is marked: 'words', 'deeds'; 'heat', 'cold'. His frantic horror of his evil is uttered in the powerful inversion 'Will all great Neptune's ocean wash this blood Clean from my hand? No, this my hand will rather The multitudinous seas incarnadine, Making the green one red'.

After the murder Macbeth's evil triumphs in chaotic emotions: 'wise', 'amazed'; 'temperate', 'furious'; 'loyal', 'neutral'; 'expedition', 'pauser'; 'violent love', 'reason'; 'silver', 'golden'; 'nature', 'ruin'; 'unmannerly breeched'. When he seeks to convince the Murderers of the necessity to kill Banquo, he sums up his persuasion with a sardonic paradox: 'sickly . . . life'; 'death . . . perfect'. Yet the torture of his life contrasts with the peace of the dead. In the banquet scene the see-saw continues: 'first', 'last'; 'without', 'within'; 'broad and general', 'cabined, cribbed, confined, bound in', and the frightful reversal of life and death, 'The time has been . . . rise again' (III. iv, 78–80). Hecate prepares destruction for him, paradoxically 'security' is 'chiefest enemy', and this is substantiated by the second and third apparitions.

In the last act Macbeth's enemies describe him as shrunk—a 'giant's robe' to a 'dwarfish thief', 'weeds' as distinct from a 'sovereign flower'. In his fury he savagely wishes evil on the boy —'black', 'cream-faced', but he realizes his own portion as 'curses' in place of 'love' and 'honour'. 'Tomorrow', 'yesterdays'; 'death', 'life'; 'candle', 'shadow', all signify nothing; 'flying hence' or 'tarrying here' is impossible, he awaits the final equivocation of the fiends that 'keep the word of promise to our ear, And break it to our hope'.

The usurper Macbeth sought by the 'worst means, the worst', the rightful heir found the 'grace of Grace'.

XII

IRONY

It has been said of *Macbeth* that it 'employs more powerfully and overtly than any other play the method of tragic irony'. Briefly dramatic irony arises out of a difference between facts known by the audience and what the characters, or some of them, believe them to be. Thus an audience may see that opinions expressed whether in good faith or not by one character are the reverse of the truth because of its foreknowledge of conflicting views. Dramatic irony may bring about an immediate piquancy, a tension from an impending calamity or a discordancy that disturbs. It alerts the audience to 'feel the future in the instant', and sometimes the past and present as 'lighting fools the way to dusty death'. Essentially one set of values or beliefs is superimposed on another, and the incongruity may provoke a grim derision, or more lightly a chuckle at the teasing of ignorance, an anxiety for the victim, a feeling of superiority and detachment, or even of relief at non-involvement. It can illuminate and make precise, and it can set a personal attitude into the frame of a universal dimension with vivid immediacy.

The arrival of Macbeth at the instant of Duncan's commen on the treachery of the previous Cawdor and the inability to judge characters from features has the flavour of a grim jest, it also defines Duncan's own trusting nature so that the audience may perceive at once the opposed qualities of the two men in relation to a general truth. The slight shock at the encounter quickens the sensibilities to look for latent significances.

The description of Macbeth's castle by Duncan and Banquo has been acclaimed as a masterpiece of irony. Its details—'martlet', 'guest', 'temple', 'loved mansionry', 'heaven's breath', 'procreant cradle', 'delicate' (air), oppose the thought in Lady Macbeth's words just previously uttered—'raven' 'fatal entrance', 'take my milk for gall', 'pall thee in the dunnest smoke of hell'. The sanctity of the royal guest, the natural fruitfulness which he symbolizes are clearly pictured expressing the natural order. They sharpen the horror of the reality within the castle, a horror given a sudden fearful presence by the appearance alone of the un-womaned, hell-given Lady Macbeth.

Macbeth's speech after the discovery of the murder, 'Had I but died . . . brag of' (II. iii, 84–9), is intended to deceive, but he speaks more profoundly than he realizes. Death 'an hour before this chance' would have saved him by redemption from damnation. His hypocrisy is overlapped by the image of the divine order evoked by his own words, which establishes the judgement to be accepted by the audience.

Among many other occasions of dramatic irony the following are noteworthy: the conversation between Duncan and Lady Macbeth (I. vi, 11–31), the Porter's scene (II. iii, 1–37), Macduff's courteous care for Lady Macbeth (II. iii, 76–9) and Ross's words to Macduff (IV. iii, 176–9).

XIII

PUNS

An effort of imagination is required if we are to appreciate the importance and value of the puns that Shakespeare uses so frequently. What has been regarded in recent times as the lowest form of wit, was, as Kellett has shown used with telling force by Isaiah and St. Paul, and by the Greek dramatists. Among the Elizabethans, who distinguised several different kinds of pun, it was an accepted means of showing intellectual brilliance and verbal dexterity. Shakespeare enlarges its scope: it may produce a simple jest or emphasize a point (Lady Macbeth's

> I'll gild the faces of the grooms withal
> For it must seem their guilt

is horrifyingly emphatic, it is not hysterical). It may sharpen the irony of an aside ('A little more than kin and less than kind'); it may be a flash of bitter insight (in *Romeo and Juliet*, the gay Mercutio mortally wounded says, 'ask for me tomorrow, and you shall find me a grave man'); or it may be employed in an exchange of witticisms.

Sometimes Shakespeare uses the two meanings of a word simultaneously, sometimes the word is repeated bearing a second meaning, or sometimes a word may have the meaning of a word of similar sound imposed on it (in *Love's Labour Lost* 'haud credo' is confused with 'ow'd grey doe', and in *As You Like It* 'goats' with 'Goths').

The puns in *Macbeth* are not excrescent dexterities, they spring spontaneously out of the mood or thought of the speaker to give it precision and memorable shape, or they deepen the implications of a particular situation. Even the quibbles of the Porter (II. iii, 32–5) are sharply relevant to the significance of the scene: 'made a shift to cast' can mean 'managed to vomit', or 'wrestled (with temptation) and overthrew it' or perhaps 'repented to drive out the demon that had possessed me'. Twice 'peace' (of death) is paired with 'peace' (untroubled life): once to emphasize Macbeth's torture of mind (III. ii, 20), and once in Ross's well-known reply to Macduff's inquiry (IV. iii, 178–9). Lady Macduff's misunderstanding of her son's answer, 'As birds do', to her question, 'How will you live?' makes sharp and clear the biblical allusion, and hence the innocence and grace of the boy. Ross's pun on 'deer' (IV. iii, 206) is perhaps a conventional and acceptable figure, it is left to Macduff to express intimate grief.

XIV

VERSE AND PROSE

The impact of dialogue was enhanced by its traditional verse form; it gave to the major characters an impressive grandeur, a stature larger than life. In Shakespeare's plays its range, power and flexibility are truly astounding, and he contrasts it from time to time with passages of prose almost as varied in style and form.

Shakespeare's verse is infinitely varied. He uses heroic couplets to form a stately narrative verse in *Richard II*, or two speakers can each speak a line of a couplet the second speaker making a comment on the first (*A Midsummer Night's Dream*, I. i, 194–201). A few couplets appearing in blank verse may mark an intense emotion; a single couplet may mark a wise or significant saying, or an important exit. Couplets can impart a sense of finality, of steps from which there can be no turning back. Couplets of shorter lines, however, are often mocking jingles (*Merchant of Venice*, I. i, 111–12) though they too can be impressively final (*A Midsummer Night's Dream*, V. i, 404 ff.).

The use of heroic couplets in *Macbeth* is not extensive. For the most part they mark the end of a scene, sometimes as in I. iii and iv they may occur several lines before the end of the scene. The couplets at I. iv, 48–53 emphatically announce Macbeth's villainy,

IV. iii, 209–10 drive home the good advice by a well-known aphorism, and V. v, 47–52 strengthen the impression of finality. V. iii, 9–10 suggests a desperate attempt to prop up his own courage; and the couplets separated by a single line of blank verse II. i, 60–1 and 63–4 increase suspense, though from the angle of the producer the first couplet is a convenient signal to the bell-ringer. III. iv, 135–43 (omitting 141) mark Macbeth's complete surrender to evil.

In early plays such as *Love's Labour's Lost* and *Romeo and Juliet* Shakespeare used elaborate rhyme patterns. The first words Romeo and Juliet speak to each other form the pattern of a sonnet. Such patterns employed with elaborate figures of speech are a sign of the depth and sincerity of the speakers' feelings. We are inclined to regard them as artificial and insincere, but to an Elizabethan they truly reflected the strength and complexity of the emotion described. No such devices are used in this play. The dignity and epic nature of tragedy and history plays is alien to the lyrical forms that express romantic love.

Shakespeare's blank verse can be elaborate, enriched with swiftly following metaphors, with similes and other figures of speech or tricks of style, and with mythological allusions; it can be plain and direct; or it can become exaggerated and violent in language in the description of warfare, in frenzied appeals to the heavens, and in boasting. Its rhythms can march with regular beat, or, particularly in later plays like *King Lear* and *Antony and Cleopatra*, the rhythms are infinitely varied to achieve the most subtle effects. The characters may use the kind of blank verse appropriate to the dramatic moment and not necessarily the kind consistent with what is known of them elsewhere in the play.

Ross's style of speaking in I. ii, 49–60 is a continuation of the style of the bleeding Captain, the epic style of the First Player in *Hamlet* describing the sack of Troy (II. ii, 444 ff.), it is quite un-like the restrained detached narrative with which he describes Duncan's pleasure at Macbeth's success (I. iii, 89–100).

Duncan's verse has directness, simplicity and well formulated phrases. Malcolm's has more dignity in his description of Cawdor's death and of Edward the Confessor's miraculous cures, descriptions that ennoble the speaker as well as praise the subjects of the speeches. With its occasional epigramatic touch it is brisker, more efficient and purposive.

Lady Macbeth utters swift, forthright statements, simple for the most part in imagery. Her sarcastic questioning of Macbeth, her rebukes during the banquet scene are argumentative and conversational in verse of light weight, yet are taut and tense.

Macbeth's verse has enormous range and variation; under the heat of imagination it is compacted with images and sonorous with latinisms, in discussion with the Murderers it is flexible and free from complex figures. The vision of the dagger calls forth short abrupt sentences as his mind gropes to reduce it to meaning. Then comes a change to lengthening rhythms for the two parallel climaxes, II. i, 49–56 and 56–60. Later in a surge of short linked descriptions of sleep hyperbole marks a train of hysteria (II. ii, 36–9), as does the weight of words in the 'multitudinous seas incarnadine'. His torture of the mind leads to abrupt changes of direction, sudden pauses in which he is poised as it were while his thoughts and feelings strive to come to terms. After Duncan's murder his speech 'Had I . . . brag of' (II. iii, 84–9) has a meditative solemnity evoked by its imagery and even rhythms, as if for the moment Macbeth was speaking with inspired insight. Is he for the moment acting as a chorus character? Later his soliloquies are purged of competing or fused images and attain a kind of dignity in the despair of V. v, 17–28. Its two simple almost commonplace images lead deftly to the dreadful finality of nothingness, his own valediction and memorial.

Prose is normally used by comic or low characters as befitting their rank, and by contrast with the verse spoken by the courtiers. It can present the stumbling conversation of a Dogberry or Verges, the chop-logic of Feste and Touchstone, the wit and expressiveness of Benedick and Beatrice, the passion of Shylock, and the pensive mood of Hamlet. Shakespeare's concern was always with dramatic effect.

Apart from IV. ii, 44–61 which some believe to be an addition after the hanging of Garnet, but which may be the result of alterations following objections by the Master of Revels, prose occurs on three occasions in the play. The letter (I. v, 1–12) is naturally in prose. The Porter's grumbling garrulity (II. iii, 1–18) and his cheerful display of antitheses and chop-logic (II. iii, 21–35) is a most effective contrast with the verse that precedes and the verse that follows. Its earnest comic triviality, set out as a logical statement, and its irony jar one's feelings. The prose of the sleep-walking scene befits the disordered mentality of Lady Macbeth, it lacks the controlled rhythm of verse. The Doctor's final reflective judgement (V. i, 64–72) brings back with sharp contrast the normality of verse.

It is sometimes very difficult to understand why Shakespeare changes the dialogue from verse to prose or from one style of blank verse to another. Occasionally the changes may be due to cuts, alterations or additions made to the original play, but in general the variations are deliberately designed to achieve some dramatic effect. They should not, therefore, be overlooked or lightly dismissed in study of the play.

XV

ELIZABETHAN STAGE PRACTICE AND THE PLAY

The stage conditions described in Appendix II determined to a large extent the shape of the plays, their dramatic devices, their methods and conventions.

The general lack of scenery gave the dramatist freedom to shift the scene of his play as often as he liked (*Antony and Cleopatra* has thirteen scenes in Act III), to change the scene unannounced while the actors remained on the stage (*Twelfth Night*, III. iv, begins in Olivia's orchard and ends in the street) or following an announcement (*Julius Cæsar*, III. i, 11–12; IV. ii, 51), or, where knowledge of locality was not necessary for the understanding of the plot, to place it nowhere in particular (*Macbeth*, I. ii; II. iv; III. vi), or in a place inconsistent with an earlier statement (III. vi). Quarto and Folio editions are not introduced with any statement of where they take place, and some scenes do not require it. The precise locating of every scene would distract attention from the plot; the scene is where the actors are. Such imprecision coupled with the rapid two-hour flow of the play uninterrupted by breaks for scene or costume changes helped to maintain the dramatic spell.

There are some uncertainties of staging in *Macbeth*. Is the discovery-space used for the cauldron in IV. i or for the show of kings? Alternatively, should the cauldron rise and sink through the main trap-door in the centre of the stage? Again, should the show of kings take place on the balcony or to the front or back of the stage? In V. viii, 34 the Folio stage direction, 'Exeunt fighting. Alarums, Enter Fighting, and Macbeth slaine', does not give a clear picture of what is intended. Some assume that Macbeth should be killed in the discovery-space or on the balcony, but in the latter case the stage direction would surely have been 'Enter above'. Perhaps Macduff to increase suspense gives ground before Macbeth's furious onslaught, and during their period off-stage the alarums, including the tolling of the bell, increase in tempo and volume. The killing of Macbeth to be fully effective should be done on the main stage, and Macbeth's body removed by soldiers even as Young Siward's body must have been removed (V. vii, 13 or 29), though there is no stage direction in either place. There is similarly no direction to the Murderers to remove the bodies of Banquo or Young Macduff.

The stage balcony would be used for Duncan's chamber, II. i, and for the hanging out the banners at V. v, i.

There was a similar freedom in the treatment of time. Inevitably some scenes overlapped, but Shakespeare placed scenes out

of their chronological order, he foreshortened time, or sometimes he merely obscured it. Thus there is obscurity in the accounts
of Cawdor (I. ii and iii) though some editors suspect cuts to the
original play. The sequence of time in III. iv, vi and IV. i, is unreal.
Macbeth decides to visit the Weird Sisters 'tomorrow' (III. iv,
132–3), and this he does in IV. i. He also says that he will send a
messenger to Macduff, and the reception of this messenger at
Macduff's castle together with Macduff's subsequent flight is described by Lennox in III. vi. At the earliest therefore some days
must have elapsed between III. iv and vi and in consequence
between III. iv and IV. i. Shakespeare may have deliberately
contrived this to give point to the warning of the first apparition,
and, as Muir points out, irony to IV. i, 82, but again editors
believe that alterations to the play have led to the interchanging
of IV. i and III. vi. On the stage, however, such inconsistences
pass unnoticed. No mention is made of the lapse of time between
II. iv and III. i, or between IV. iii and V. ii. In a play remarkable
for its impression of speed, the events from IV. iii onwards rush
with frightening speed to Macbeth's end.

The plays at the Theatre and the Globe took place in the afternoon and daytime was assumed in their action. Night was mentioned directly or by reference to torches, candles, or lanterns if
the action demanded it as in *A Midsummer Night's Dream*, II. i, or
as in *Macbeth*, to help create an atmosphere of horror and evil.

An important convention was the practice of the soliloquy and
the aside. The jutting out of the stage into the middle of the
theatre floor brought the actors who were well forward nearer
to the bulk of the audience than to actors at the rear of the stage.
It had long been established that character and motives were
announced directly, the audience was not left to guess what was
going on in a character's mind. It was a simple matter, therefore,
for an actor to come forward out of earshot of the others on the
stage and reveal confidentially to the audience his character, his
motives and his intentions. In this way Shylock declared his

villainy, Cassius his intention to seduce Brutus, and Brutus his agonizing inner struggle. This device linked actor and audience intimately: the spectators shared in the play, they had a god-like knowledge of the hearts of the characters, and the two things increased their feelings of tension and suspense and the moments of dramatic irony.

Macbeth does speak this kind of soliloquy (I. iv, 48–53), but he more often meditates aloud, his thoughts coming unevenly and tortuously in the act of creation; he speaks to himself rather than to the audience. This, foreshadowed perhaps by some of the soliloquies of Brutus in *Julius Cæsar,* is a new phase in Shakespeare's development as a dramatist, and it may well owe something to the demoniac influences on Macbeth.

The brief, pointed aside which gave the audience a kind of nudge to remind them of some matter, and which also maintained a close intimacy between actor and audience, occurred only once at V. iii, 61–2 where the Doctor expresses a wish to escape from Dunsinane.

Macbeth demanded considerable use of effects and stage properties. Thunder and lightning by rolling cannon balls over hollow wooden floors and stairs and by firing gunpowder accompanied the witches. Trap-doors, probably three in number were used by the Witches, the Apparitions and Banquo, and for the cauldron. A car or chariot on pulleys may have raised Hecate moonwards into billowy material representing clouds (III. v, 34–5). In addition to military equipment, banners, drums, trumpets, a banqueting service was needed, and torches, oboes, bells and Macbeth's head.

The ornate stage, the magnificent costumes, the royal and noble characters produced an element of formal pageantry in the performance of the plays. Gesture and stage business were formal, dignified and restricted and the emphasis was placed on the delivery of the speeches. To an audience accustomed to the impressive oratory of preachers at St. Paul's Cross, to sustained and eloquent speaking by its notabilities trained in rhetoric, the words of a play were particularly important. A well-spoken passage of rich word painting reporting, for example, some event that had happened off stage was rousing and satisfying. It was a kind of pageantry in speech or as a Jacobean writer put it, 'an ampullous and scenical pomp' of words.

MACBETH

CHARACTERS

DUNCAN, King of Scotland
MALCOLM ⎫
DONALBAIN ⎬ his sons
MACBETH ⎫
BANQUO ⎬ generals of the King's army
MACDUFF ⎫
LENNOX │
ROSS │
MENTEITH ⎬ noblemen of Scotland
ANGUS │
CAITHNESS ⎭
FLEANCE, son to Banquo
SIWARD, Earl of Northumberland, general of the English forces
YOUNG SIWARD, his son
SEYTON, an officer attending on Macbeth
BOY, son to Macduff
AN ENGLISH DOCTOR
A SCOTTISH DOCTOR
A CAPTAIN
A PORTER
AN OLD MAN
LADY MACBETH
LADY MACDUFF
GENTLEWOMAN attending on Lady Macbeth
THREE WITCHES
HECATE
APPARITIONS
Lords, Gentlemen, Officers, Soldiers, Murderers, Attendants,
and Messengers
SCENE: *Scotland; England*

An open place

Should the witches 'enter' on the balcony, in the discovery space, on the open stage, or through the trap-doors assisted by thunder and lightning?

S.D.   *Thunder and lightning.* Such disturbances in the heavens were thought to indicate rebellion in kingdoms, strife in the minds of men, and the loosing abroad of the forces of evil. *three Witches.* Macbeth and Banquo call them 'weyward sisters'. They are servants and forms of evil; should they therefore be hideous, plain or glamorous? Should their voices be thin and high, gruff and grating, snarling or eager, chanting or speaking? Should their movements be stately, furtive, rhythmic, stylized or patterned?

3   *hurlyburly's*, fighting's, rebellious struggle's.

4   *When . . . won.* A riddling forecast thought by some to anticipate a fight for Macbeth's soul as well as the victory at Fife.

8   *Greymalkin*, Greycat. A spirit in animal shape, a familiar, was supposed to be given by Satan to a witch to help her sorcery, and to summon her to meetings.

      What grouping and movements are appropriate here?

9   *Paddock*, Toad. Another familiar.

10   *Anon*, coming!

11–12   *Fair . . . air.* A calling upon evil to overturn ideas of good and bad, to confuse the false appearance with the reality, to distort nature. Perhaps also a hint that a human soul, well known to be both fair and foul, is to be assaulted and its reason clouded by mists of evil. See the morality play *Wisdom*, l. 157, 'a soul is both foul and fair', and Woolton, *Immortality of the Soul*, 1576, 'the devil addeth his poison . . . casting a thick dim mist in the vertue intellective !'

12   *Hover*, A suggestion of a brooding evil presence.

      What purpose has this scene: merely to announce the time of the next meeting of the witches, to create a sinister, foreboding atmosphere; to amuse the groundlings or interest King James; to arouse suspense, doubt, ambiguity, contradiction; or to introduce obscurely as a prologue-cum-dumbshow themes of the play?

      Does the rhyme suggest or underline an incantation, an invocation, a circle of evil, or a pattern to match movement?

38

ACT ONE

SCENE ONE

Thunder and lightning. Enter three WITCHES

FIRST WITCH: When shall we three meet again
  In thunder, lightning, or in rain?
SECOND WITCH: When the hurlyburly's done,
  When the battle's lost and won.
THIRD WITCH: That will be ere the set of sun.
FIRST WITCH: Where the place?
SECOND WITCH: Upon the heath.
THIRD WITCH: There to meet with Macbeth.
FIRST WITCH: I come Greymalkin!
SECOND WITCH: Paddock calls.
THIRD WITCH: Anon!   10
ALL: Fair is foul, and foul is fair;
  Hover through the fog and filthy air.   [*Exeunt*

A camp near the battlefield

A brisk entry with banners immediately on the alarm call.

S.D   *Alarum within*, i.e. a battle trumpet blast although the battle is elsewhere. This sudden blast accompanied by drums and rapid action and the bleeding Captain, is a sharp contrast to the first scene. *bleeding Captain*. Is he alone, accompanied, or helped by Duncan's bodyguard?

1–3   *What . . . state*. Duncan's words 'bloody man' link the revolt with 'battle' in the first scene.

       bloody. 'Blood' is mentioned or implied over a hundred times in the play.

3–7   *This . . . it*. What qualities in Malcolm does his first speech suggest —generosity, leadership, courage, popularity, manliness?

3   *sergeant*. Elsewhere referred to as Captain. Rank was not always precisely distinguished in Shakespeare's time, nor in Shakespeare: Bardolph in *Henry V* varies from corporal to lieutenant.

4–5   *Who . . . captivity*. Stage tradition presents Malcolm wounded as if from an earlier stage of the battle.

       How should Malcolm recognize and greet the Captain?

8   *spent*, exhausted.

9   *art*, ability to swim.

11–12 *multiplying . . . him*, (*a*) the evils in his nature breed as fast as lice or (*b*) the ever increasing evil spirits gather to his side (i.e. for revenge on Macbeth) (Paul).

13   *kerns*, lightly armed Irish foot soldiers. *gallowglasses*, Irish horse soldiers.

14   *fortune*. Fortune was depicted as a woman blindfold on a moving sphere or wheel. Her fickleness in bestowing favours or disasters was well-known. *on . . . smiling*, favouring his accursed cause.

15   *whore*, mistress. See *Hamlet*, II, ii, 230–1. *But . . . weak*, i.e. fortune and the rebel army.

18   *smoked*, steamed with blood.

19   *minion*, favourite.

20   *Till . . . slave*. Some editors believe that a cut in the original text has occurred here; others that the exhaustion of the speaker demands a pause. See ll. 35–42.

21   *Which . . . him*. A grim jest.

22   *nave*, navel. *chops*, jaws.

      The Captain's style has been called bombastic, overdone, epic,

SCENE TWO

Alarum within. Enter DUNCAN, MALCOLM, DONALBAIN, LENNOX, *with* ATTENDANTS, *meeting a bleeding* CAPTAIN

DUNCAN: What bloody man is that? He can report,
  As seemeth by his plight, of the revolt
  The newest state.
MALCOLM: This is the sergeant
  Who like a good and hardy soldier fought
  'Gainst my captivity. Hail brave friend.
  Say to the King the knowledge of the broil
  As thou didst leave it.
CAPTAIN: Doubtful it stood,
  As two spent swimmers, that do cling together
  And choke their art. The merciless Macdonwald—
  Worthy to be a rebel, for to that   10
  The multiplying villainies of nature
  Do swarm upon him—from the Western Isles
  Of kerns and gallowglasses is supplied,
  And fortune on his damned quarrel smiling
  Showed like a rebel's whore. But all's too weak,
  For brave Macbeth—well he deserves that name—
  Disdaining fortune, with his brandished steel,
  Which smoked with bloody execution,
  Like valour's minion carved out his passage,
  Till he faced the slave;   20
  Which ne'er shook hands, nor bade farewell to him,
  Till he unseamed him from the nave to th' chops,
  And fixed his head upon our battlements.
DUNCAN: O valiant cousin, worthy gentleman!

heroic, and likened to the Pyrrhus speech in *Hamlet*, and to the speeches of messengers in Seneca's tragedies. Should any gestures accompany the speech?

How do Duncan and his courtiers receive the news?

25   *reflection*, (*a*) shining, (*b*) turning back at the spring equinox.

26   *direful*, terrible.

27–8 *So . . . swells*, (*a*) so from the east, the well-known source of heavenly grace, further perils threaten, (*b*) so from the east, at the coming of the pleasant springtime, further perils threaten.

27   *spring*, (*a*) source, (*b*) day-spring.

28   *Mark*. Where was Duncan's attention?

29   *No . . . armed*, i.e. the courage of the king's forces in their just cause.

30   *skipping*, light-footed, prancing. Contemptuous.

31   *Norweyan lord*, Sweno, king of Norway. *surveying vantage*, seeing an opportunity.

32   *furbished*, well-polished, well-prepared.

33   *Dismayed*, put to flight.

34–42 As above l. 20 the Captain's pauses for breath or for stabs of pain may account for the irregular lines.

Does the Captain enjoy telling his tale, or is he appalled or fascinated with horror?

36   *sooth*, truth.

37   *with double cracks*, i.e. with double charges of powder.

40   *memorize another Golgotha*, make the battlefield as memorable as the 'place of the skull'. *Golgotha*. A word of horrifying significance.

46   *haste*, urgency.

47   *seems to*, is about to.

How are the characters grouped on the stage to focus attention on Ross?

God . . . King. Is this—triumphant, formal, ominous, anxious?

Ross's account overlaps that of the Captain.

CAPTAIN: As whence the sun 'gins his reflection
Shipwrecking storms and direful thunders break,
So from that spring, whence comfort seemed to come,
Discomfort swells. Mark King of Scotland, mark.
No sooner justice had, with valour armed,
Compelled these skipping kerns to trust their heels,   30
But the Norweyan lord, surveying vantage,
With furbished arms, and new supplies of men,
Began a fresh assault.
DUNCAN: Dismayed not this
Our captains, Macbeth and Banquo?
CAPTAIN: Yes,
As sparrows eagles, or the hare the lion.
If I say sooth, I must report they were
As cannons overcharged with double cracks, so they
Doubly redoubled strokes upon the foe.
Except they meant to bathe in reeking wounds,
Or memorize another Golgotha,   40
I cannot tell—
But I am faint, my gashes cry for help.
DUNCAN: So well thy words become thee as thy wounds,
They smack of honour both. Go get him surgeons.

                          [*Exit Captain, attended*
                    Enter ROSS *and* ANGUS
Who comes here?
MALCOLM: The worthy Thane of Ross.
LENNOX: What a haste looks through his eyes! So
should he look
That seems to speak things strange.
ROSS: God save the King!

49   *flout*, mock, insult. The present tense perhaps serves to emphasize the great fear the Scots felt at first, and so to enhance the magnitude of the victory.

50   *fan . . . cold*, turn our people cold with fear.

53   *dismal*, fearful, terrible.

54   *Bellona's bridegroom*, i.e. Macbeth. In Roman myth Bellona was the goddess of war. *lapped in proof*, clad in armour.

55   *confronted . . . self-comparisons*, matched him (Sweno) on equal terms at every point, sword point against sword point, his arm against the rebel's arm.

57   *lavish*, wild, insolent.

58   *Great happiness*. Any gesture, or movement among courtiers?

60   *craves composition*, begs for terms of peace.

62   *Saint Colme's Inch*, Inchcomb, an island in the Firth of Forth.

63   *dollars*, silver coins, originally Dutch, in circulation in Elizabethan times.

64   *that*. Should this be emphasized?

65   *bosom interest*, intimate trust. *present*, immediate.

66   *former title*. See l. 52. Is there any ominous undertone? *greet*, (*a*) welcome, (*b*) 'great' vb = make great. (Hulme).

68   *lost . . . won*. The play abounds in oppositions of this kind. Is this an echo of I. i, 4?

       Is this scene intended—to show Macbeth as the saviour of the realm from the horror of rebellion and invasion, to depict or satirize the savage brutality of war, to sharpen suspense in the light of the evil threat of I. i?

A heath

An entry similar to that of I. i.

2   *Killing swine*. For the accomplishments of the witches see Introduction p. 6.

DUNCAN: Whence camest thou, worthy Thane?

ROSS: From Fife, great King,
    Where the Norweyan banners flout the sky,
    And fan our people cold. Norway himself,   50
    With terrible numbers,
    Assisted by that most disloyal traitor,
    The Thane of Cawdor, began a dismal conflict,
    Till that Bellona's bridegroom, lapped in proof,
    Confronted him with self-comparisons,
    Point against point, rebellious arm 'gainst arm,
    Curbing his lavish spirit; and to conclude,
    The victory fell on us.

DUNCAN: Great happiness!

ROSS: That now
    Sweno, the Norways' King, craves composition.   60
    Nor would we deign him burial of his men
    Till he disbursed, at Saint Colme's Inch,
    Ten thousand dollars to our general use.

DUNCAN: No more that Thane of Cawdor shall deceive
    Our bosom interest. Go pronounce his present death,
    And with his former title greet Macbeth.

ROSS: I'll see it done.

DUNCAN: What he hath lost noble Macbeth hath won.

                                              [*Exeunt*

SCENE THREE

Thunder. Enter three WITCHES

FIRST WITCH: Where hast thou been, sister?

SECOND WITCH: Killing swine.

THIRD WITCH: Sister, where thou?

FIRST WITCH: A sailor's wife had chestnuts in her lap,
    And munched, and munched, and munched—'Give me,'
        quoth I.

6   *Aroint*, be off, get out. *rump-fed*, (*a*) pampered with the best
     joints, or (*b*) fat-bottomed. *ronyon*, scabby wretch.
7   *Tiger*. See note to l. 22.

10   *I'll do*, i.e. having slipped on board she will take revenge on the
     master of the ship.
        Any gestures?

14   *other*, others.
15   *ports they blow*, either (*a*) 'they' = 'ports' or (*b*) 'from' is under-
     stood after 'blow'.
16   *quarters*, i.e. of the compass.
17   *shipman's card*, sailor's compass card, or sailor's chart.

20   *penthouse lid*, eyelid or eyebrow. A penthouse was a lean-to shed
     with a sloping roof.
21   *forbid*, accursed.
22   *Weary . . . nine*. A ship named the *Tiger* put in at Milford Haven
     on 27 June, 1606, after a disastrous voyage during which her
     master was killed. Her voyage was the subject of gossip in
     London. Loomis points out that her voyage lasted exactly 'sev'n-
     nights nine times nine'.
23   *peak*, waste away.
s.d. *drum*. Dramatically most effective to announce Macbeth's first
     appearance even though he and Banquo are unattended.

33   *Posters*, swift travellers.
34   *go about*. In dancing in a ring witches held hands and faced out-
     wards.
37   *wound up*, (*a*) by their windings, (*b*) an ominous suggestion of a
     trap that is set.
        What dramatic purpose does the account of the Master of the
     Tiger serve—to show the vengeful nature and power of the
     witches, to score a topical hit, to foreshadow what will befall
     Macbeth who is also going homeward, to enlarge the idea of
     witchcraft in time and place?
38   *so . . . seen*. Does this link Macbeth with the witches by echoing
     I. i, 11–12? Is it a reference to contrasting weather—the witches
     being obscured in fog of their own making? Is 'fair' a reference
     to the victory?

'Aroint thee witch,' the rump-fed ronyon cries.
Her husband's to Aleppo gone, master o' th' *Tiger*;
But in a sieve I'll thither sail,
And like a rat without a tail,
I'll do, I'll do, and I'll do.   10
SECOND WITCH: I'll give thee a wind.
FIRST WITCH: Th' art kind.
THIRD WITCH: And I another.
FIRST WITCH: I myself have all the other,
And the very ports they blow,
All the quarters that they know
I' the shipman's card.
I'll drain him dry as hay;
Sleep shall neither night nor day
Hang upon his penthouse lid.   20
He shall live a man forbid;
Weary sev'n-nights nine times nine
Shall he dwindle, peak, and pine.
Though his bark cannot be lost,
Yet it shall be tempest-tossed.
Look what I have.
SECOND WITCH: Show me, show me.
FIRST WITCH: Here I have a pilot's thumb,
Wrecked as homeward he did come.   [*Drum within*
THIRD WITCH: A drum, a drum!   30
Macbeth doth come.
ALL: The Weird Sisters, hand in hand,
Posters of the sea and land,
Thus do go about, about,
Thrice to thine, and thrice to mine,
And thrice again, to make up nine.
Peace, the charm's wound up.
                    Enter MACBETH *and* BANQUO
MACBETH: So foul and fair a day I have not seen.

47

39   *How ... Forres?* Is this spoken to Macbeth or to the silent witches?

39–42 *What ... on't?* Any movement or gesture?

40–2 *So ... on't,* i.e. their appearance is unnatural and unearthly.

42   *Live you,* i.e. are you creatures of flesh and blood?

42–3 *aught ... question,* are you spirits whom it is not forbidden to question? (See IV. i, 75.)

44–5 *By ... lips,* i.e. the witches have come to meet Macbeth not Banquo.

44   *choppy,* chapped, cracked.

46   *beards.* Sometimes found on witches. (See *Merry Wives,* IV. ii, 169–71.)

48   *All hail.* Elsewhere Shakespeare associates this greeting with Judas Iscariot, hence it may have here a sinister and treacherous undertone.

      Any gesture or movement?

51–2 *why ... fair?* Have the witches touched on Macbeth's secret longings, is he afraid of the evil he senses, or that his own schemes are to be revealed; or do the prophecies start in human evil though not imagined before?

      How does Macbeth show fear?

53   *fantastical,* imaginary.

55–6 *present ... hope.* A reference to the three titles—Glamis, Cawdor, and King.

57   *rapt,* (*a*) carried away from himself, in a trance, with a fixed, glazed look, (*b*) implicated (Folio 'wrapt'). A hint of the imagery of 'borrowed robes' (Hulme).

58   *seeds of time.* The growth of spirit and matter in nature was thought to spring from seeds hidden in the earth by God. Evil spirits had some power to foretell how these seeds would develop. See IV. i, 59.

60–1 *who ... hate.* Banquo firmly proclaims his integrity.

65–7 *Lesser ... none.* Again the contradictions and confusions.

67   *get,* beget, be the ancestor of.

BANQUO: How far is't called to Forres? What are these,
So withered, and so wild in their attire,   40
That look not like th' inhabitants o' th' earth,
And yet are on't? Live you, or are you aught
That man may question? You seem to understand me,
By each at once her choppy finger laying
Upon her skinny lips. You should be women,
And yet your beards forbid me to interpret
That you are so.
MACBETH: Speak if you can. What are you?
FIRST WITCH: All hail Macbeth, hail to thee, Thane of Glamis!
SECOND WITCH: All hail Macbeth, hail to thee, Thane of
Cawdor!
THIRD WITCH: All hail Macbeth, that shalt be King here-
after!   50
BANQUO: Good sir, why do you start, and seem to fear
Things that do sound so fair? I' th' name of truth
Are ye fantastical, or that indeed
Which outwardly ye show? My noble partner
You greet with present grace, and great prediction
Of noble having, and of royal hope,
That he seems rapt withal. To me you speak not.
If you can look into the seeds of time,
And say which grain will grow, and which will not,
Speak then to me, who neither beg nor fear   60
Your favours nor your hate.
FIRST WITCH: Hail!
SECOND WITCH: Hail!
THIRD WITCH: Hail!
FIRST WITCH: Lesser than Macbeth, and greater.
SECOND WITCH: Not so happy, yet much happier.
THIRD WITCH: Thou shalt get kings, though thou be none.
So all hail Macbeth and Banquo!
FIRST WITCH: Banquo and Macbeth, all hail!

70   *Stay.* What are the witches doing? *imperfect speakers*, speakers who
       have not told all.
71   *Sinel's*, i.e. Macbeth's father's.
72–3   *The . . . gentleman.* Does Macbeth not know that Cawdor helped
       Sweno (I. ii, 52–7) and has been sent to execution (see ll. 112–16).
       Has Shakespeare in condensing Holinshed made a slip, or is
       Macbeth lying to test the witches, or has the text been altered?
74   *prospect of belief*, view of what may be believed.
76   *owe*, have. *strange*, (*a*) surprising, (*b*) unearthly. *intelligence*, news.
78   *charge*, command.

80   *of them*, of the same nature. *Wither . . . vanished.* The witches dis-
       appear in the smoke.
81   *corporal*, of solid flesh.
82   *Would . . . stayed.* Banquo is interested in what the witches were,
       Macbeth in what they said.
84   *insane root.* Probably the root of the plant henbane said to cause
       hallucinations when eaten.
85   *That . . . prisoner*, that takes from the mind its powers of thinking
       clearly.
86–8   *Your . . . words.* Is this spoken jokingly, reflectively, or with
       pretended indifference?
87   *Thane . . . too.* Does Macbeth mimic the witches?
88   *To . . . words.* A quibble on 'went' in a musical sense (Wilson).

91   **venture**, perilous actions. *rebels' fight*, i.e. against Macdonwald.
92–3   *His . . . his*, his mind is at a loss whether to express praise of your
       deeds or his own amazement at them.
93   *that*, i.e. the struggle in his mind.

97   *Strange . . . death*, unnatural forms of death.
97–8   *hail Came.* The Folio has 'Tale Can'. Some editors print 'tale
       Came', taking 'as . . . tale' to mean 'as fast as they could be
       counted', 'tale' = 'tally'. Mrs. Hulme suggests 'tale' = 'spoken
       word'.

MACBETH: Stay you imperfect speakers, tell me more.   70
  By Sinel's death I know I am Thane of Glamis,
  But how of Cawdor? The Thane of Cawdor lives
  A prosperous gentleman; and to be king
  Stands not within the prospect of belief,
  No more than to be Cawdor. Say from whence
  You owe this strange intelligence, or why
  Upon this blasted heath you stop our way
  With such prophetic greeting? Speak, I charge you.
                              [Witches vanish
BANQUO: The earth hath bubbles, as the water has,
  And these are of them. Whither are they vanished?   80
MACBETH: Into the air; and what seem'd corporal melted
  As breath into the wind. Would they had stayed.
BANQUO: Were such things here as we do speak about?
  Or have we eaten on the insane root
  That takes the reason prisoner?
MACBETH: Your children shall be kings.
BANQUO: You shall be King.
MACBETH: And Thane of Cawdor too; went it not so?
BANQUO: To th' selfsame tune and words. Who's here?

Enter ROSS *and* ANGUS

ROSS: The King hath happily received, Macbeth,
  The news of thy success; and when he reads   90
  Thy personal venture in the rebels' fight,
  His wonders and his praises do contend,
  Which should be thine or his. Silenced with that,
  In viewing o'er the rest o' th' selfsame day,
  He finds thee in the stout Norweyan ranks,
  Nothing afeard of what thyself didst make,
  Strange images of death. As thick as hail
  Came post with post, and every one did bear
  Thy praises in his kingdom's great defence,

102   *herald*, lead you with honour.

104   *for . . . honour*, i.e. the title of Thane of Cawdor. The words, how-
        ever, recall the third prophecy of the witches. *earnest*, pledge.
106   *addition*, title.

107   *Can . . . true?* Banquo realizes the evil nature of the witches. The
        Devil was notoriously the father of lies, *St. John*, viii, 44.
108–9   *dress . . . robes*. The frequency of images relating to clothes has
        been noted in this play.
109   *borrowed*, not my own.
110   *heavy judgement*, sentence of death.

112   *line*, support, reinforce.
113   *vantage*, benefit.
114   *in . . . wrack*, to bring about the ruin of his country.
115   *capital*, punishable by death.
117   *The . . . behind*. How should this be said—exultantly, wonderingly,
        unbelievingly, with conviction?
           Any movement here and in the following line?
118–   *Do . . . them?* Is this to test Banquo's feelings towards the witches'
   20   prophecy, or out of his good fortune to share his happiness?

120   *home*, utterly, completely.
121   *enkindle you*, rouse a desire in you for.
122–6   *But . . . consequence*. Is this an aside or spoken to Macbeth? This was
        a very important matter, Lavater, *Of Ghosts and Spirits*, pp. 171–4,
        devotes a whole chapter to it.
123   *to . . . harm*, to persuade us.
124   *instruments of darkness*, i.e. devils, witches, 'murdering ministers',
        'metaphysical aid'.
127   *Cousins . . . you*. Is this a crude device or an attempt to draw
        attention from Macbeth who has become 'rapt'? *Two . . . told*. An
        ironic echo of Banquo's 'tell us truths'.

And poured them down before him.

ANGUS: We are sent 100

To give thee from our royal master thanks,
Only to herald thee into his sight,
Not pay thee.

ROSS: And for an earnest of a greater honour,
He bade me, from him, call thee Thane of Cawdor;
In which addition, hail most worthy Thane,
For it is thine.

BANQUO: [*Aside*] What, can the devil speak true?

MACBETH: The Thane of Cawdor lives. Why do you dress me
In borrowed robes?

ANGUS: Who was the Thane lives yet,
But under heavy judgement bears that life 110
Which he deserves to lose. Whether he was combined
With those of Norway, or did line the rebel
With hidden help and vantage, or that with both
He laboured in his country's wrack, I know not;
But treasons capital, confessed and proved,
Have overthrown him.

MACBETH: [*Aside*] Glamis, and Thane of Cawdor.
The greatest is behind. [*To Ross and Angus*] Thanks for your
  pains.
[*To Banquo*] Do you not hope your children shall be kings,
When those that gave the Thane of Cawdor to me
Promised no less to them?

BANQUO: That, trusted home, 120
Might yet enkindle you unto the crown,
Besides the Thane of Cawdor. But 'tis strange:
And oftentimes, to win us to our harm,
The instruments of darkness tell us truths,
Win us with honest trifles, to betray's
In deepest consequence.
Cousins, a word I pray you.

128 *swelling act*, majestic play, unfolding drama.
129 *I . . . gentlemen*. An absent-minded courtesy.
130 *supernatural soliciting*, trafficking with spirits.

131 *Cannot . . . good*. The short line may indicate pauses and gestures—
     evil to the left, good to the right. Macbeth in morality play
     fashion is weighing the opposing virtue and vice.
134–7 *why . . . nature?* Why do I give way to that inner prompting to a
     deed so horrifying to think of that my hair stands on end.
137 *use of nature*, natural beating. *fears*, things causing fear.
139– *My . . . not*, my thought, in which murder is yet merely an unreal
  42   idea, so disturbs the harmony of my being that my powers of
     action are overwhelmed by my imaginings, and nothing exists
     for me except my thought which has no reality.

140 *single . . . man*, i.e. the kingdom of man, the microcosm. See note
     to I. i, s.d.

142 *Look . . . rapt*. Is this said calmly, amusedly, inquiringly or
     anxiously? *rapt*, absorbed by an idea and unconscious of surround-
     ings.
145 *strange*, foreign, new.
145–6 *cleave . . . use*, do not fit until they have been worn.
145 *mould*, (*a*) model, (*b*) human body.

146–7 *Come . . . day*. Macbeth decides to let things take their course.
     The couplet emphasizes the proverbial summing up.

149 *favour*, forgiveness. *wrought*, troubled, overwrought.
150 *things forgotten*. Is this a lie?
151 *registered . . . them*, i.e. in the book and volume of my brain, or
     perhaps the book of memory.
154 *The interim*, in the meantime. *weighed*, considered.
155 *Our free hearts*, freely our inmost thoughts.
     Macbeth's greatness in others' eyes, his present confession of
     temptation, inner struggle and fears, skilfully involves the
     audience in what is happening to him rather than what may
     happen to Duncan.

MACBETH: [*Aside*]   Two truths are told
  As happy prologues to the swelling act
  Of the imperial theme.—I thank you gentlemen.—
  [*Aside*] This supernatural soliciting   130
  Cannot be ill, cannot be good.
  If ill, why hath it given me earnest of success,
  Commencing in a truth? I am Thane of Cawdor.
  If good, why do I yield to that suggestion,
  Whose horrid image doth unfix my hair,
  And make my seated heart knock at my ribs,
  Against the use of nature? Present fears
  Are less than horrible imaginings.
  My thought, whose murder yet is but fantastical,
  Shakes so my single state of man, that function   140
  Is smothered in surmise, and nothing is
  But what is not.
BANQUO: Look how our partner's rapt.
MACBETH: [*Aside*] If chance will have me King, why chance
    may crown me
  Without my stir.
BANQUO: New honours come upon him,
  Like our strange garments, cleave not to their mould
  But with the aid of use.
MACBETH: [*Aside*]   Come what come may,
  Time and the hour runs through the roughest day.
BANQUO: Worthy Macbeth, we stay upon your leisure.
MACBETH: Give me your favour: my dull brain was wrought
  With things forgotten. Kind gentlemen, your pains   150
  Are registered where every day I turn
  The leaf to read them. Let us toward the King.
  [*To Banquo*] Think upon what hath chanced, and at more
    time,
  The interim having weighed it, let us speak
  Our free hearts each to other.

Forres

A formal, ceremonial entry. Are any stage properties required—a chair, throne, etc?

2   *in commission*, commanded to do it.

8   *Became him*, was more fitting.
9   *had been studied*, had rehearsed his part. In Shakespeare's day men, publicly executed, took pains in their bearing and their last speech to leave an impression of courage and dignity.
10   *owed*, possessed.
11–12 *There's . . . face*, there is no method of discovering the way a man thinks from the appearance of his face.

     Macbeth's entry during this speech turns it to irony. Why is this mention of Cawdor introduced at all—to lead up to the irony of Macbeth's entry, to score a topical hit (See Appendix), to set a standard of repentance in death by which to judge Macbeth's death later, to present Malcolm in a favourable light by giving him a generous epitaph to speak over a traitor?

15–16 *sin . . . me*. A sharp contrast with the sin that was heavy on Macbeth 'even now'.
19–20 *That . . . mine*, that I could have offered you thanks and reward in equal proportion.

BANQUO: Very gladly.
MACBETH: Till then enough.—Come friends.

[*Exeunt*

SCENE FOUR

Flourish. Enter DUNCAN, MALCOLM, DONALBAIN, LENNOX,
and ATTENDANTS

DUNCAN: Is execution done on Cawdor? Are not
Those in commission yet returned?
MALCOLM: My liege,
They are not yet come back. But I have spoke
With one that saw him die; who did report
That very frankly he confessed his treasons,
Implored your Highness' pardon, and set forth
A deep repentance. Nothing in his life
Became him like the leaving it; he died
As one that had been studied in his death,
To throw away the dearest thing he owed, 10
As 'twere a careless trifle.
DUNCAN: There's no art
To find the mind's construction in the face.
He was a gentleman on whom I built
An absolute trust.

Enter MACBETH, BANQUO, ROSS, *and* ANGUS
O worthiest cousin,
The sin of my ingratitude even now
Was heavy on me. Thou art so far before,
That swiftest wing of recompense is slow
To overtake thee. Would thou hadst less deserved,
That the proportion both of thanks and payment

21 *More . . . pay.* An ironical statement. *all*, all I possess.

22–7 *The . . . honour.* Is Macbeth sincere, overcome by Duncan's grac
guilty, strained, hypocritical?

28–9 *I . . . growing.* Should he embrace Macbeth?

32–3 *There . . . own.* A courteous quibble.
33–4 *plenteous, Wanton, fulness.* Words associated with 'harvest' and
crops.

34 *Wanton*, luxuriant.
How does Duncan display his tearfulness? Any pause?
35–9 *Sons . . . Cumberland.* The overthrow of Scotland's enemies by
Macbeth ironically leads Duncan to declare Malcolm his heir. He
thus secures the succession, but puts an obstacle in Macbeth's way.
Some editors think that this sudden change of subject is due to
the cutting of some passages. Cumberland was then held by
Scotland on conditions from the English crown.
41–2 *signs . . . deserves.* Perhaps a last minute allusion to the investment
of King Christian with the Order of the Garter.
41 *signs*, marks of honour.

45 *harbinger*, forerunner.

Might have been mine. Only I have left to say, 20
More is thy due than more than all can pay.
MACBETH: The service and the loyalty I owe,
In doing it pays itself. Your Highness' part
Is to receive our duties; and our duties
Are to your throne and state, children and servants,
Which do but what they should by doing every thing
Safe toward your love and honour.
DUNCAN: Welcome hither.
I have begun to plant thee, and will labour
To make thee full of growing. Noble Banquo,
That hast no less deserved, nor must be known 30
No less to have done so. Let me infold thee,
And hold thee to my heart.
BANQUO: There if I grow,
The harvest is your own.
DUNCAN: My plenteous joys,
Wanton in fulness, seek to hide themselves
In drops of sorrow. Sons, kinsmen, Thanes,
And you whose places are the nearest, know,
We will establish our estate upon
Our eldest, Malcolm, whom we name hereafter
The Prince of Cumberland; which honour must
Not unaccompanied invest him only, 40
But signs of nobleness, like stars, shall shine
On all deservers. From hence to Inverness,
And bind us further to you.
MACBETH: The rest is labour, which is not used for you.
I'll be myself the harbinger, and make joyful
The hearing of my wife with your approach;
So humbly take my leave.
DUNCAN: My worthy Cawdor.
MACBETH: [*Aside*] The Prince of Cumberland—that is a step,
On which I must fall down, or else o'erleap,

50–1 *Stars . . . desires.* See I. v, 48–52 and II. i, 4–5.

52 *wink at*, see not. *be*, be done.
53 *Which . . . fears.* See II. ii, 52, 54–5, 59.
    The sudden apparent frustration of Macbeth's hopes rouses his
    evil desires.
54 *he*, i.e. Macbeth. *so*, as you say.
55–6 *in . . . me*, i.e. Duncan is so generous that the praise of others is
    meat and drink to him.
    What qualities does Duncan show—generosity, sensitiveness,
    tearfulness, innocence, grace, duty, gratitude, courtesy?

Macbeth's castle

Is this, Lady Macbeth's first entry, furtive, slow, impressive, sinister,
hasty, impetuous?

Does she open the letter on the stage, or has she opened it beforehand?
Should her voice be low or high, curt or drawling? Her speech demands
considerable variation in speed and intonation.

2 *perfect'st report*, best sources of information.

5 *missives*, messengers.

7–8 *referred . . . time*, indicated the future to me.
8 *Hail . . . be!* How should this be said—with exaltation, wonder,
    unbelief, fiendish joy?
10 *dues of rejoicing*, anything of what should give you joy.
11–12 *Lay . . . heart*, think earnestly about this.
    Does Lady Macbeth lay the letter to her heart?
13–14 *and . . . promised.* Is this spoken with decision, awe, ecstasy, power?
15 *milk . . . kindness*, (a) mild gentleness, (b) weak, wishy-washy
    sentimentality.
    Is this said scornfully, naturally, sarcastically, sneeringly?
16 *catch . . . way*, take the direct path. Politely grim.
17–20 *Art . . . win.* Macbeth's virtues are vices in Lady Macbeth's view.
    She points out the contradictions in Macbeth's mind.
18 *illness . . . it*, evil that must accompany it.

For in my way it lies. Stars hide your fires,   50
Let not light see my black and deep desires.
The eye wink at the hand; yet let that be,
Which the eye fears when it is done to see.   [*Exit.*
DUNCAN: True worthy Banquo; he is full so valiant,
  And in his commendations I am fed;
  It is a banquet to me. Let's after him,
  Whose care is gone before to bid us welcome.
  It is a peerless kinsman.   [*Flourish. Exeunt*

SCENE FIVE

Enter LADY MACBETH, *reading a letter*

LADY MACBETH: 'They met me in the day of success; and I have
  learned by the perfect'st report, they have more in them than
  mortal knowledge. When I burned in desire to question them
  further, they made themselves air, into which they vanished.
  Whiles I stood rapt in the wonder of it, came missives from
  the King, who all-hailed me "Thane of Cawdor", by which
  title, before these weird sisters saluted me, and referred me
  to the coming on of time with "Hail King that shalt be!"
  This have I thought good to deliver thee, my dearest partner
  of greatness, that thou mightst not lose the dues of rejoicing
  by being ignorant of what greatness is promised thee. Lay it to
  thy heart, and farewell.'   12
Glamis thou art, and Cawdor, and shalt be
What thou art promised; yet do I fear thy nature,
It is too full o' th' milk of human kindness
To catch the nearest way. Thou wouldst be great,
Art not without ambition, but without
The illness should attend it. What thou wouldst highly,

21   *That, it,* the crown.

22–3 *that . . . undone,* i.e. the murder.

23   *Hie,* hasten, come quickly.

24   *pour . . . ear,* i.e. and so flood his whole being. See *Hamlet* I. v, 62–7.

25   *chastise,* whip, lash. *valour,* boldness.

26   *round,* crown.

27   *metaphysical,* supernatural. *doth seem,* appears to promise.
      Is the Messenger hurried, formal or leisurely? See l. 34.

29   *Thou . . . it.* Is this—concern as a hostess caught unprepared or shock at the leap of events making the murder imminent?
      Walker suggests that in view of the last few lines Lady Macbeth for a moment thinks the servant refers to Macbeth as king, and that her secret thought is betrayed. She therefore tries to cover her exclamation by the not very convincing explanation, ll. 30–1.
      Any action by Lady Macbeth?

35   *Give him tending,* take care of him.

36–8 *The . . . battlements,* the raven itself, whose voice foretells disaster and death, would be so certain of death about to befall Duncan that it would croak itself hoarse.

38   *my.* Should this be stressed?

38–9 *spirits . . . thoughts,* evil spirits that wait to enter a human mind when that mind shows willingness to receive them.
      Should Lady Macbeth pause before calling on the spirits? Should she kneel, stand or make any movement or gesture?

39   *mortal thoughts,* (*a*) thoughts of death, (*b*) human thoughts. *unsex me here.* Harsh and forced.

41   *direst,* bitterest, fiercest.

41–2 *make . . . remorse,* curdle my blood so that the flow of vital spirits in it is stopped, and no messages may reach my heart to stir up pity.

43   *compunctious . . . nature,* natural impulses of pity.

44   *fell,* fierce, cruel.

44–5 *nor . . . it,* nor put peace like a barrier between my purpose and its fulfilment.

46   *take . . . gall,* (*a*) put gall in the place of my milk, or (*b*) drink my milk which has turned to gall. Gall was thought to promote rage and malice. *ministers,* spirits.

That wouldst thou holily; wouldst not play false,
And yet wouldst wrongly win. Thou'dst have, great Glamis,
That which cries 'Thus thou must do, if thou have it';   21
And that which rather thou dost fear to do
Than wishest should be undone. Hie thee hither,
That I may pour my spirits in thine ear,
And chastise with the valour of my tongue
All that impedes thee from the golden round,
Which fate and metaphysical aid doth seem
To have thee crowned withal.

Enter ATTENDANT
                              What is your tidings?
MESSENGER: The King comes here tonight.
LADY MACBETH: Thou'rt mad to say it.
  Is not thy master with him, who were't so   30
  Would have informed for preparation.
MESSENGER: So please you, it is true; our Thane is coming.
  One of my fellows had the speed of him
  Who almost dead for breath, had scarcely more
  Than would make up his message.
LADY MACBETH: Give him tending,
  He brings great news.   [*Exit attendant*
                        The raven himself is hoarse
  That croaks the fatal entrance of Duncan
  Under my battlements. Come you spirits
  That tend on mortal thoughts, unsex me here,
  And fill me from the crown to the toe top-full   40
  Of direst cruelty; make thick my blood,
  Stop up th' access and passage to remorse,
  That no compunctious visitings of nature
  Shake my fell purpose, nor keep peace between
  Th' effect and it. Come to my woman's breasts,
  And take my milk for gall, you murd'ring ministers,

48   *wait . . . mischief*, further the unnatural horrors in nature.

49   *pall*, wrap as in a corpse covering or as a robe for tragedy. *dunnest*, darkest.

50–2 *That . . . hold.* Did Lady Macbeth intend to murder Duncan herself, or is this a fearful imagining of the murder of the sleeping Duncan in advance?

      Is Macbeth's entry sudden, impressive, dignified, startling, breathless, affectionate?

      Should Lady Macbeth move or make any gesture—kneel or place her hands on his shoulders?

53   *all-hail hereafter.* A dramatically effective link with the witches' words whether they were in Macbeth's letter or not.

54–6 *Thy . . . instant.* See ll. 52–3.

55   *ignorant present*, this present time which knows nothing of the greatness to come.

57   *Duncan . . . tonight.* How spoken—rapidly, urgently, hesitantly, deliberately savouring each word, stealthily? *And . . . hence?* How spoken—sharply, ominously, with a stress on 'goes hence' to point a double meaning?

58–9 *O . . . see*, i.e. may the day that he will go away never dawn. Has the dialogue so far been without implication, and does this so shock Macbeth that he reveals his feelings?

60–1 *Your . . . matters.* Any movement or gesture from Lady Macbeth?
      book . . . matters. Perhaps a hint at books of strange studies such as necromancy, witchcraft and sorcery.

61   *beguile the time*, deceive the world.

62   *Look . . . time*, let your behaviour fit the occasion.

63–4 *look . . . under't.* A well-known image used elsewhere by Shakespeare. Its appearance in emblem form on a medallion struck to celebrate the detection of Gunpowder Plot—a feat attributed to James—may have recalled it to Shakespeare.

64   *He that's coming.* What effect has the avoidance of the name?

65   *provided for.* A grim quibble.

66   *my dispatch.* Is Lady Macbeth intending to commit the murder or to set the stage for it? *dispatch*, (*a*) management, (*b*) putting to death.

68   *solely*, wholly, 'for us alone' (Groom).

69   *We . . . further.* Is Macbeth uneasy, in full agreement, or asserting his position as head of the house?

Wherever in your sightless substances
You wait on nature's mischief. Come thick night,
And pall thee in the dunnest smoke of hell,
That my keen knife see not the wound it makes,   50
Nor heaven peep through the blanket of the dark,
To cry 'Hold, hold!'

Enter MACBETH

                          Great Glamis, worthy Cawdor,
Greater than both, by the all-hail hereafter,
Thy letters have transported me beyond
This ignorant present, and I feel now
The future in the instant.
MACBETH: My dearest love.
Duncan comes here tonight.
LADY MACBETH: And when goes hence?
MACBETH: Tomorrow, as he purposes.
LADY MACBETH: O never
Shall sun that morrow see.
Your face, my Thane is as a book where men   60
May read strange matters. To beguile the time,
Look like the time; bear welcome in your eye,
Your hand, your tongue; look like th' innocent flower,
But be the serpent under't. He that's coming
Must be provided for; and you shall put
This night's great business into my dispatch,
Which shall to all our nights and days to come
Give solely sovereign sway and masterdom.
MACBETH: We will speak further.
LADY MACBETH: Only look up clear;

70 *To . . . fear*, to show that unusual expression will make men think you have something fearful on your mind. *favour*, looks, expression.

How should they leave the stage—Lady Macbeth urging Macbeth with her hands, leading him by the hand, separately?

At the entrance of the castle

S.D. *Oboes and torches.* Why are these required?

1 *seat*, situation.
2 *Nimbly*, lightly-stirring. *sweetly*, freshly.
3 *gentle senses*, gentle to our senses.
4 *temple-haunting martlet*, house-martin that frequents holy places. Some think that 'guest' and 'martlet' (martin) point to Duncan. 'Martin'=a dupe, one who is tricked. *approve*, prove.
5 *mansionry*. Folio has 'mansonry'. Some editors prefer 'masonry'.
6 *jutty*, part that juts out or overhangs.
7 *coign of vantage*, suitable corner.
8 *pendent*, i.e. clinging to the wall. *procreant cradle*, nest for its young.
10 *delicate*, soft, mild.

These two speeches express thoughts of soft-air, love, breeding, and holiness. Do they derive any effect from following (*a*) the fog and filthy air of I. i, 12, (*b*) Lady Macbeth's unsexing and rejection of breeding, (*c*) Lady Macbeth's invoking of night's thick murk, (*d*) the murderous intentions of the Macbeths?

After Lady Macbeth's last words 'Leave all the rest to me' tension rises as she, and not Macbeth, greets Duncan. One famous actress entered here clad completely in red.

11–14 *The . . . trouble*, the love that surrounds me sometimes causes me to be troubled, but yet I am thankful because it is love. In this way I show you how you can pray God to regard me for the trouble my visit gives you (because it springs from my loving regard for you).

Perhaps a courtly compliment. What dramatic effect has the fearful irony?

15 *double*, (*a*) twice, (*b*) two-faced.
16 *single*. This also means 'weak'.

To alter favour ever is to fear   70
Leave all the rest to me.   [*Exeunt*

SCENE SIX

Oboes and torches. Enter DUNCAN, MALCOLM, DONALBAIN,
BANQUO, LENNOX, MACDUFF, ROSS, ANGUS, *and*
ATTENDANTS

DUNCAN: This castle hath a pleasant seat; the air
  Nimbly and sweetly recommends itself
  Unto our gentle senses.
BANQUO: This guest of summer,
  The temple-haunting martlet, does approve,
  By his loved mansionry, that the heavens' breath
  Smells wooingly here. No jutty, frieze,
  Buttress, nor coign of vantage, but this bird
  Hath made his pendent bed and procreant cradle.
  Where they most breed and haunt, I have observed
  The air is delicate.
                Enter LADY MACBETH
DUNCAN: See, see our honoured hostess.   10
  The love that follows us sometime is our trouble,
  Which still we thank as love. Herein I teach you,
  How you shall bid God 'ild us for your pains,
  And thank us for your trouble.
LADY MACBETH: All our service
  In every point twice done, and then done double,
  Were poor and single business to contend
  Against those honours deep and broad wherewith

18   *house*, family.

20   *We . . . hermits*, we shall pray continually for you our benefactor.
      Lady Macbeth takes up Duncan's reference to prayer. In view of
      Lady Macbeth's evil prayers I. v, is this hypocritical, gloating,
      strained, overdone?

22   *purveyor*, an officer who went ahead of the king to provide for his
      accommodation and food.

23   *great . . . spur*. Macbeth's spur was of another kind. See I. vii, 25–8.

25   *your*. Perhaps emphatic. Recall I. v, 60–70.

26   *compt*, account.

28   *Still*, always.

31   *By . . . hostess*. Does Duncan take her hand, kiss her or bow her off
      the stage?
          Duncan's speeches here, as in I. ii, are full of grace and love.
      What dramatic value has the emphasis on the 'hostess' and
      'guest'?

A room in the castle

Are any properties required?

S.D.   *Sewer*, (*a*) official food taster, (*b*) attendant who superintended the
        serving of food.

          What is the point of this procession of servants—to give atmos-
        phere and information, to hint at a 'last supper' from which Judas
        (Macbeth) goes apart (*St. John*, xiii. 27, 30)?

1–8   *If . . . here*, if the deed were done with the moment it is committed,
       then it would be well to do it quickly. If the act of murder could
       hold in check any unpleasant consequences and secure success with
       his death, so that this one blow might be all that is necessary and
       the end of the whole matter here.

3   *trammel*, (*a*) net, hobble (a horse), (*b*) bind up a corpse (Hulme).

4   *his surcease*, (*a*) Duncan's death, or (*b*) prevention of the con-
       sequences. *success*, (*a*) happy result, (*b*) succession (to the throne).
       See *Winter's Tale*, I. ii, 394.

5–6   *here, But here*. The pause and repetition of 'here' marks the break-
       ing in of a train of thought implied by 'here'.

Your Majesty loads our house. For those of old,
And the late dignities heaped up to them,
We rest your hermits.

DUNCAN: Where's the Thane of Cawdor?   20
We coursed him at the heels, and had a purpose
To be his purveyor; but he rides well,
And his great love, sharp as his spur, hath holp him
To his home before us. Fair and noble hostess,
We are your guest tonight.

LADY MACBETH: Your servants ever
Have theirs, themselves, and what is theirs, in compt,
To make their audit at your Highness' pleasure,
Still to return your own.

DUNCAN: Give me your hand.
Conduct me to mine host, we love him highly,
And shall continue our graces towards him.   30
By your leave hostess.   [*Exeunt*

SCENE SEVEN

Oboes and torches. Enter a SEWER, *and divers* SERVANTS *with
dishes and service, and pass over the stage. Then enter* MACBETH

MACBETH: If it were done, when 'tis done, then 'twere well
It were done quickly. If th' assassination
Could trammel up the consequence, and catch
With his surcease, success; that but this blow
Might be the be-all and the end-all—here,
But here, upon this bank and shoal of time,

Macbeth

6   *bank . . . time.* Theobald's emendation for the Folio reading 'Banke and Schoole of time'. The spelling 'school' or 'scole' was also used for 'shoal'. Some writers regard 'bank' as a judicial bench and retain school pointing out the continuance of the thought in 'cases', 'judgement', 'instructions' and 'justice', ll. 7–10.

7   *jump,* evade, risk. *cases,* (a) matters, (b) law suits.

8   *that,* in that.

9–10 *return . . . inventor,* recoil on the head of the originator of the crime.

10   *even-handed,* fair, well-balanced.

11   *Commends,* presents. *ingredience,* ingredients. *poisoned chalice.* A hint of contradiction—'chalice' has religious associations.

14   *Strong,* i.e. strong reasons.

17   *borne . . . meek,* exercised his powers so gently.

18   *clear,* blameless.

18–20 *virtues . . . taking-off.* A reminiscence of the morality plays.

19   *plead like angels,* i.e. in the court of Heaven.

20   *deep damnation,* deadly sin.

21–5 *pity . . . wind,* Duncan's virtues like the helplessness and tenderness of a naked baby and the innocence and grace of a cherub will rouse pity that will over-ride with the sanctity of love the blast of accusation, and will cause universal weeping. (See Helen Gardner, *The Profession of a Critic*, pp. 53–61).

22   *blast,* i.e. storm of horror and grief.

22–3 *cherubin . . . air.* Perhaps an echo of *Psalms*, xviii. 10.

23   *sightless . . . air,* winds. *sightless,* invisible, unseen.

24–5 *shall . . . wind,* i.e. the coming of rain lessens the force of the wind that brings it. See *3 Henry VI*, I. iv, 143–6; *Troilus and Cressida*, IV. iv, 52–3, for a similar comparison.

26   *To . . . intent,* to urge on my purpose. See *Twelfth Night*, 'My purpose is indeed a horse of that colour' (II. iii, 153).

27–8 *Vaulting . . . other,* impetuous ambition like (a) a rider who jumps over his horse and falls down on the other side, or (b) a rider who puts his horse too fiercely at a jump and both fall on the other side.

    Macbeth uses the arguments against the murder that the good angel of a morality play might have used; the rough justice that others might kill him, the crime against social morality and the curse of Cain, the universal horror and grief at sin against Heaven.

We'd jump the life to come. But in these cases
We still have judgement here, that we but teach
Bloody instructions, which being taught return
To plague th' inventor. This even-handed justice   10
Commends th' ingredience of our poisoned chalice
To our own lips. He's here in double trust:
First, as I am his kinsman and his subject,
Strong both against the deed; then, as his host,
Who should against his murderer shut the door,
Not bear the knife myself. Besides, this Duncan
Hath borne his faculties so meek, hath been
So clear in his great office, that his virtues
Will plead like angels, trumpet-tongued against
The deep damnation of his taking-off.   20
And pity, like a naked new-born babe,
Striding the blast, or heaven's cherubin, horsed
Upon the sightless couriers of the air,
Shall blow the horrid deed in every eye,
That tears shall drown the wind. I have no spur
To prick the sides of my intent, but only
Vaulting ambition, which o'erleaps itself,
And falls on th' other—

Macbeth

Lady Macbeth's entry is swift and urgent, and an apt contradiction of Macbeth's statement 'I have no spur'. Her speaking demands a wide range of speed, pitch and inflection.

30   *Know . . . has*, i.e. frequently.
32   *bought*, won.
34   *would*, ought to be. *gloss*, (*a*) brightness, (*b*) favourable meaning.
36   *dressed*. Lady Macbeth scornfully takes up Macbeth's image, 'worn . . . aside.'
37   *to . . . pale*, i.e. with a hangover (Muir).
39   *Such*, i.e. so changeable.
39–41   *Art . . . desire*, are you afraid to match your desires with your deeds and courage. The contrast between action and desire is frequent in the play. See II. iii, 24–31.
42   *ornament of life*, i.e. the crown.
45   *cat i' th' adage*, i.e. the cat wanted to eat fish but would not wet her feet. *adage*, proverb.
47   *is none*, (*a*) there is no man who dares do more, (*b*) is not a man (but is superhuman or devilish. Wilson). *beast*, An insulting contrast with 'man'.
     Lady Macbeth neatly turns Macbeth's boast by referring to the current view of the scale of existence.
48   *That . . . me*. Is this evidence of a cut scene (see I. v. 71), or a discussion preceding the play, a lie, sufficiently explained by Macbeth's letter, a device to blacken Macbeth lest he should appear spineless, a reference back to give the effect of depth, Lady Macbeth speaking as a personification of Macbeth's evil will? *break*, mention.
50, 51   *more, more the man*. Echoes of ll. 46–7. So far Lady Macbeth reinforces her rejection of Macbeth's remark by distorting his words, now she rounds off the matter with this quibble, 'unmake', i.e. unman.
52   *Did then adhere*, were then convenient.
54   *I . . . suck*. To his wavering manhood she opposes her womanhood to embarrass him.
54–5   *know . . . me*. Is this true womanly tenderness, calculated tactics, ruthless hypocrisy after I. v, 45–6?

Enter LADY MACBETH

How now? What news?

LADY MACBETH: He has almost supped. Why have you left
the chamber?

MACBETH: Hath he asked for me?

LADY MACBETH: Know you not he has?   30

MACBETH: We will proceed no further in this business.
He hath honoured me of late, and I have bought
Golden opinions from all sorts of people,
Which would be worn now in their newest gloss,
Not cast aside so soon.

LADY MACBETH: Was the hope drunk
Wherein you dressed yourself? Hath it slept since?
And wakes it now to look so green and pale
At what it did so freely? From this time
Such I account thy love. Art thou afeard
To be the same in thine own act and valour   40
As thou art in desire? Wouldst thou have that
Which thou esteem'st the ornament of life,
And live a coward in thine own esteem,
Letting 'I dare not' wait upon 'I would,'
Like the poor cat i' th' adage?

MACBETH: Prithee peace.
I dare do all that may become a man;
Who dares do more is none.

LADY MACBETH: What beast was't then,
That made you break this enterprise to me?
When you durst do it, then you were a man;
And to be more than what you were, you would   50
Be so much more the man. Nor time nor place
Did then adhere, and yet you would make both.
They have made themselves, and that their fitness now
Does unmake you. I have given suck, and know

73

56–9   *I . . . this.* Is this mercilessness, honourable oath-keeping, playing her womanhood against Macbeth's manhood?

59   *We fail?* It seems best to keep the Folio lineation and punctuation, although a question mark in the Folio sometimes stands where we should use an exclamation mark. Support has been given to 'We fail', and 'We fail!'

60   *screw . . . sticking-place,* i.e. as the string of a viol or of a crossbow is screwed up.

64   *wassail,* drinking. *convince,* overcome.

65–6   *memory . . . fume.* The brain was described as having four chambers in one of which was memory. It was believed that fumes from liquors rose to the brain and caused drunkenness.

66–7   *the . . . only,* the chamber of reason, like the receiver of the still, will become a mere 'retort in which the crude undistilled liquids bubble and fume' (Schanzer).

67   *limbeck,* retort. *swinish,* i.e. since their reason was overcome by wine, and animals lacked human reason.

68   *drenched,* (*a*) drowned, (*b*) 'medicined' like beasts.

    Walker suggests the fusing of two parallel descriptions, the guards at the entrance to the divine king's chamber, and memory guarding the entrance to the chamber of reason in the brain.

71   *spongy,* drunken.

72   *quell,* kill. *Bring . . . only.* Ironic and enthusiastic.

73   *mettle,* (*a*) spirit, (*b*) substance (metal).

74   *received,* accepted.

77   *other,* otherwise.

78–9   *we . . . death,* we will be loud in our outcries and lamentations over his death.

79   *bend up,* make tense as the frame of a bow.

80   *corporal agent,* bodily power.

81   *mock the time,* deceive all the world.

81–2   *mock . . . know.* See I. v, 62–5. Macbeth echoes his wife's insistence on maintaining false appearances.

    In this scene Macbeth is a figure like the Mankind of a morality play. Lady Macbeth, his bad angel, attacks his pride of valour and his scruples and presents a plan of action. The virtuous side, however, coming from his own mouth involves the audience with him.

How tender 'tis to love the babe that milks me—
I would while it was smiling in my face
Have plucked my nipple from his boneless gums,
And dashed the brains out, had I so sworn as you
Have done to this.

MACBETH:　　　　　If we should fail?

LADY MACBETH:　　　　　　　　We fail?
But screw your courage to the sticking-place,　　　　60
And we'll not fail. When Duncan is asleep—
Whereto the rather shall his day's hard journey
Soundly invite him—his two chamberlains
Will I with wine and wassail so convince,
That memory, the warder of the brain,
Shall be a fume, and the receipt of reason
A limbeck only; when in swinish sleep
Their drenched natures lie as in a death,
What cannot you and I perform upon
Th' unguarded Duncan? What not put upon　　　　70
His spongy officers, who shall bear the guilt
Of our great quell?

MACBETH:　　　　　Bring forth men-children only,
For thy undaunted mettle should compose
Nothing but males. Will it not be received,
When we have marked with blood those sleepy two
Of his own chamber, and used their very daggers,
That they have done't?

LADY MACBETH:　　　　Who dares receive it other,
As we shall make our griefs and clamour roar
Upon his death?

MACBETH:　　　　I am settled, and bend up
Each corporal agent to this terrible feat.　　　　80
Away, and mock the time with fairest show:
False face must hide what the false heart doth know. [*Exeunt*

75

A courtyard in the castle

1–3   *How . . . sir.* A careful marking of the passing of the night.

2–5   *moon . . . out.* An ominous sign. See I. iv, 50; v, 48–52.

4   *husbandry,* thrift.

5   *that.* Perhaps sword-belt.

6   *summons,* i.e. call to sleep. *lead.* A glance at the leaden mace of Morpheus, the god of sleep.

7–9   *Merciful . . . repose.* Banquo pleads with the Powers, an order of angels to drive away the demons that cause him to have evil dreams.

14   *largess,* gifts of money. *offices,* servants' quarters.

15   *diamond.* The diamond was reputed to protect its owner against witchcraft and terror by night.

16   *shut up,* (*a*) finished the day, (*b*) wrapped in.

17–19   *Being . . . wrought,* because we were unprepared, our wishes to offer freely of our hospitality were limited by our shortcomings.

18–19   *will, defect, free.* An ominous quibble: 'free will' in christian belief was enslaved through defect to the powers of evil.

20   *I . . . Sisters.* Perhaps the 'cursed thoughts', l. 8.

21   *I . . . them.* Is Macbeth tense, afraid to think of the witches, alarmed, suspicious?

ACT TWO

SCENE ONE

Enter BANQUO, *and* FLEANCE *bearing a torch before him*

BANQUO: How goes the night, boy?
FLEANCE: The moon is down; I have not heard the clock.
BANQUO: And she goes down at twelve.
FLEANCE: I take't, 'tis later sir.
BANQUO: Hold, take my sword. There's husbandry in heaven,
Their candles are all out. Take thee that too.
A heavy summons lies like lead upon me,
And yet I would not sleep. Merciful powers,
Restrain in me the cursed thoughts that nature
Gives way to in repose. Give me my sword.
        Enter MACBETH, *and a* SERVANT *with a torch*
Who's there?   10
MACBETH: A friend.
BANQUO: What sir, not yet at rest? The king's a-bed.
He hath been in unusual pleasure, and
Sent forth great largess to your offices.
This diamond he greets your wife withal,
By the name of most kind hostess, and shut up
In measureless content.
MACBETH: Being unprepared,
Our will became the servant to defect,
Which else should free have wrought.
BANQUO: All's well,
I dreamt last night of the three Weird Sisters.   20
To you they have showed some truth.
MACBETH: I think not of them.

77

23   *We would*, you and I should. Or is it a royal 'we' by anticipation?

25   *cleave . . . consent*, (*a*) follow my advice, (*b*) be one of my supporters. *when 'tis*, (*a*) when the time comes, (*b*) when we have our
talk.

26   *honour*, i.e. rewards and titles. *none*, i.e. honourable character.

26–7 *lose . . . augment*. A contradictory expression.

28   *franchised*, free from guilt. *clear*, unstained.
  What value has this episode—to introduce Fleance, to pass the
time, to give Macbeth a chance to draw back, to show that
Banquo under pressure of evil still resists?

31–2 *when . . . bell*. The signal for the murder. Is this spoken naturally
or with deliberation? Some action or stage business is called for
during the pause before Macbeth resumes speaking.

33–4 *Is . . . hand?* Should Macbeth show horror, fear or confidence? Is
this a warning, an hallucination, an incitement created by evil
powers?
  Lavater, *Of Ghosts and Spirits*, p. 92 notes that spirits have appeared
as 'an instrument, as a staff, a sword . . . which the spirit held in his
hand'.

34–5 *Come . . . still*. Actions should be carefully dignified.

36   *fatal*, ominous, foreboding. *sensible*, capable of being grasped by
the senses.

38   *false*, unreal

39   *heat-oppressed brain*, i.e. mind disordered by unbalanced humours.

41   *As . . . draw*. The short line perhaps is to allow for action. Is the
unsheathing slow or suddenly resolute?

42   *marshall'st . . . going*. The dagger appears to turn towards Duncan's
bedroom.

44–5 *Mine . . . rest*, my eyes are deceiving me if my other senses are
correct, or else they see correctly and are more reliable than the
rest of the senses together.
  Any movement or gesture?

46   *dudgeon*, handle. *gouts*, drops.

48–9 *informs Thus*, creates this shape.

50   *Nature seems dead*, (*a*) all action seems to have ceased, (*b*) all natural
things seem dead. *wicked dreams abuse*, i.e. unnatural things.

Yet when we can entreat an hour to serve,
We would spend it in some words upon that business,
If you would grant the time.
BANQUO: At your kind'st leisure.
MACBETH: If you shall cleave to my consent, when 'tis,
It shall make honour for you.
BANQUO: So I lose none
In seeking to augment it, but still keep
My bosom franchised, and allegiance clear,
I shall be counselled.
MACBETH: Good repose the while.
BANQUO: Thanks sir, the like to you.   30
                    [*Exeunt Banquo and Fleance*
MACBETH: Go bid thy mistress, when my drink is ready,
She strike upon the bell. Get thee to bed.   [*Exit servant*
Is this a dagger which I see before me,
The handle toward my hand? Come let me clutch thee.
I have thee not, and yet I see thee still.
Art thou not, fatal vision, sensible
To feeling as to sight? Or art thou but
A dagger of the mind, a false creation,
Proceeding from the heat-oppressed brain?
I see thee yet, in form as palpable   40
As this which now I draw.
Thou marshall'st me the way that I was going,
And such an instrument I was to use.
Mine eyes are made the fools o' th' other senses,
Or else worth all the rest. I see thee still;
And on thy blade and dudgeon gouts of blood,
Which was not so before. There's no such thing.
It is the bloody business which informs
Thus to mine eyes. Now o'er the one half-world
Nature seems dead, and wicked dreams abuse   50

51   *curtained sleep.* An allusion to (*a*) the curtains round four-poster beds, (*b*) eyelids. See *Tempest*, I. ii, 408.

51–2   *Witchcraft . . . offerings.* Hecate in classical myth and in later times was the goddess of the witches, noted for her destructive powers and for her power of granting every mortal his heart's desire. *offerings,* i.e. ceremonies, rituals, heart's desire.

53   *wolf.* Associated with murder in the classical legend of Lycaon, who for murder was changed into a wolf.

54   *his watch,* his (i.e. wolf's) watchword or clock. Murder is told of the passage of the night by the wolf's howl.

55   *Tarquin's ravishing strides.* Tarquinius Sextus, son of an early Roman king, violated Lucretia, the wife of Collatine, a noble Roman. She killed herself. See Shakespeare's *Rape of Lucrece.*

56–8   *Thou . . . whereabout.* These lines have echoes of several passages from the Bible: the foundation of the earth (*Psalms* 93. 2) the steps, walking in the way (frequently), the stones talking (*St. Luke*, xix. 40, and with closer resemblances to the context *Habbakuk*, ii. 10–12, 20 (Muir)). Is this a reminder that in spite of the release of evil, ll. 50–6, God's design still endures?

59   *And . . . time,* i.e. (*a*) the stones will betray him and lessen the horror by breaking the silence and the tension, (*b*) the stones will catch in their tones the fearful horror of this moment.

61   *Words . . . gives,* i.e. to blow into the flame of action.

    After Macbeth's stealthy footsteps the sudden stroke of the bell is an almost unbearable shock.

    Is Macbeth's soliloquy—due to a trance-like condition, an abnormal mind, or a bewitched mind, an attempt to drive away his good instincts, to remind the audience of the unnaturalness of the crime? How should he leave—trance-like, furtively, firmly as on a reeling deck, gropingly, with a leg left lingering in the door of the bedroom?

The same

Lady Macbeth enters closely on Macbeth's exit.

1–2   *That . . . fire.* Is this a reminder of the plan (I. vii, 63–72), a sign of strain, or a recurrence of the theme of contradiction?

3   *fatal bellman.* In May 1605, Robert Dow gave money to pay for a bellman to ring his bell outside Newgate Prison on the night before the execution of a condemned prisoner to prepare him for death.

The curtained sleep; witchcraft celebrates
Pale Hecate's offerings; and withered murder,
Alarumed by his sentinel the wolf,
Whose howl's his watch, thus with his stealthy pace,
With Tarquin's ravishing strides, towards his design
Moves like a ghost. Thou sure and firm-set earth,
Hear not my steps, which way they walk, for fear
Thy very stones prate of my whereabout,
And take the present horror from the time,
Which now suits with it. Whiles I threat, he lives: 60
Words to the heat of deeds too cold breath gives.

[A bell rings

I go, and it is done. The bell invites me.
Hear it not Duncan, for it is a knell
That summons thee to heaven or to hell.   *[Exit*

SCENE TWO

Enter LADY MACBETH

LADY MACBETH: That which hath made them drunk hath
     made me bold;
  What hath quenched them hath given me fire. Hark! Peace!
  It was the owl that shrieked, the fatal bellman,

4–6   *He . . . snores.* What movement or action leads to these discoveries?

5   *grooms,* i.e. of the bedchamber.

6   *charge,* duty of guarding the King. *possets.* Hot drinks of milk curdled with wine to which was added sugar, eggs, and spices.

9   *Who's there.* The Folio gives Macbeth an entry at this point. Some suggest that he appears for a moment on the balcony, but perhaps the direction merely means, as Wilson notes, that Macbeth speaks inside the bedchamber—an effective touch.

10–12   *Alack . . . us.* Should Lady Macbeth show alarm, sorrow, annoyance, or resignation?

11–12   *attempt . . . us.* Macbeth thought otherwise. See I. vii, 1–25.

12   *Confounds,* overthrows, defeats.

13–14   *Had . . . done't.* Is this a reminder of Duncan's royal father-figure, a glimpse of Lady Macbeth's womanly nature, an anticipation of the horror of her return to the chamber, a sign that she intended to murder Duncan herself?

S.D.   *Enter Macbeth.* Should he rush out wildly daggers uplifted, creep out stealthily, or walk as in a trance? Accordingly how should he speak?

15–20   *Didst . . . Donalbain.* Macbeth at first fears discovery.

21   *sorry,* miserable, wretched.

25   *addressed them,* made themselves ready.

26   *There . . . together,* i.e. Malcolm and Donalbain.

Which gives the stern'st good night. He is about it.
The doors are open; and the surfeited grooms
Do mock their charge with snores. I have drugged their
    possets,
That death and nature do contend about them,
Whether they live or die.
MACBETH: [*Within*] Who's there? What ho!
LADY MACBETH: Alack, I am afraid they have awaked,   10
And 'tis done. Th' attempt and not the deed
Confounds us. Hark! I laid their daggers ready,
He could not miss 'em. Had he not resembled
My father as he slept, I had done't.

Enter MACBETH

          My husband!
MACBETH: I have done the deed. Didst thou not hear a noise?
LADY MACBETH: I heard the owl scream and the crickets cry.
  Did not you speak?
MACBETH: When?
LADY MACBETH: Now.
MACBETH: As I descended?
LADY MACBETH: Ay.
MACBETH: Hark!
  Who lies i' th' second chamber?
LADY MACBETH: Donalbain.   20
MACBETH: This is a sorry sight.   [*Looks on his hands*
LADY MACBETH: A foolish thought, to say a sorry sight.
MACBETH: There's one did laugh in's sleep, and one cried
    'Murder!'
  That they did wake each other. I stood and heard them.
  But they did say their prayers, and addressed them
  Again to sleep.
LADY MACBETH: There are two lodged together.

27–8   *One . . . hands*, i.e. out of fear and terror.
28   *hangman's hands*, i.e. bloodstained from taking out the heart of
       the victim he had quartered.

32–3   *I . . . throat*. This may glance at Macbeth's bewitching, since
       inability to say a prayer was a sign of a witch or sorcerer. Any
       gesture?
32   *I . . . blessing*. A grim realization of loss of grace.
33–4   *These . . . mad*. An ironic reversal of ll. 11–12.
35   *Sleep no more*. So Sisson who suggests that only 'Sleep no more'
       should be included on both occasions, the rest is Macbeth's appalled
       comment. Editors vary very much in what they attribute to the
       voice here and in ll. 41–3.
37   *knits . . . sleave*, brings order to the tangle threads of silk.
38   *death*, ending in rest.
39   *second course*, (*a*) second life-process (wakefulness being the first),
       (*b*) meat course at dinner.
41   *Still*, continually.
42–3   *Glamis . . . more*. Is this an external voice or the imaginary voice
       of conscience mingling with the prophecies of the witches.
44   *Who . . . cried*. Is she scornful or bewildered?

45   *unbend*, give way. See I. vii, 79–80.
46   *brainsickly*. Contemptuous. See V. iii, 40 where Macbeth applies
       'mind diseased' to Lady Macbeth.
47   *witness*, evidence.

52   *Look . . . not*. Is this fear of his own thoughts or of the corpse? He
       takes refuge in 'it' for 'him'. *Infirm*, sickly, wavering.
53   *Give . . . daggers*. Perhaps she wrenches them from his clenched
       grasp.
53–4   *The . . . pictures*, i.e. both alike are mere pictures of the living
       person.

MACBETH: One cried 'God bless us!' and 'Amen!' the other,
As they had seen me with these hangman's hands.
Listening their fear, I could not say 'Amen,'
When they did say 'God bless us!'

LADY MACBETH: Consider it not so deeply.   30

MACBETH: But wherefore could not I pronounce 'Amen'?
I had most need of blessing, and 'Amen'
Stuck in my throat.

LADY MACBETH: These deeds must not be thought
After these ways; so, it will make us mad.

MACBETH: Methought I heard a voice cry 'Sleep no more!'
Macbeth does murder sleep, the innocent sleep,
Sleep that knits up the ravelled sleave of care,
The death of each day's life, sore labour's bath,
Balm of hurt minds, great nature's second course,
Chief nourisher in life's feast.

LADY MACBETH: What do you mean?   40

MACBETH: Still it cried 'Sleep no more!' to all the house.
Glamis hath murdered sleep, and therefore Cawdor
Shall sleep no more, Macbeth shall sleep no more.

LADY MACBETH: Who was it that thus cried? Why worthy
    Thane,
You do unbend your noble strength, to think
So brainsickly of things. Go get some water,
And wash this filthy witness from your hand.
Why did you bring these daggers from the place?
They must lie there. Go carry them, and smear
The sleepy grooms with blood.

MACBETH: I'll go no more.   50
I am afraid to think what I have done.
Look on't again I dare not.

LADY MACBETH: Infirm of purpose!
Give me the daggers. The sleeping and the dead
Are but as pictures. 'Tis the eye of childhood

54–5 *'tis . . . devil*, i.e. only a child is afraid of a mere picture of a devil.

55 *painted*, (a) coloured, (b) bloodstained, See *Henry V*, III. v, 49; *Troilus and Cressida*, I. i, 90; *King John*, IV. ii, 253.

56 *gild*, (a) paint, (b) redden. Gold was regarded as 'red'.

57 *guilt*. Is the pun mocking, grim, hysterical, resolute, emphatic, or clinching?

58 *How . . . me?* Does he not appreciate the reality of the knocking?

59 *What . . . eyes*. A possible echo of *St. Matthew*, xviii. 9. See Introduction, p. 20.

60–3 *Will . . . red*. Commentators suggest that this may be an unconscious reminiscence of passages in Seneca's plays. It may also echo *Revelation*. See Introduction, p. 21.

62 *incarnadine*, dye blood-red.

63 *Making . . . red*, (a) making red the green sea, or, (b) making the green sea totally red. The Folio comma after 'one' suggests that (a) is preferable.

64 *your*, i.e. of your hands.

65 *wear*, carry, show.

67 *A . . . deed*. An ironic comment on ll. 60–3.

68–9 *Your . . . unattended*, your self-control has deserted you. Perhaps an ironic glance at Macbeth's loss of loyalty.

71 *watchers*, i.e. still awake.

72 *poorly*, lacking in spirit, dejectedly.
    Is Lady Macbeth pleading, urging, coaxing or commanding?

73 *To . . . myself*, (a) I had rather remain lost in my thoughts than have to face up to my crime, or less likely, (b) if I have to face up to my crime, it is best for me to reject the self that did it.

74 *Wake . . . couldst*. Is he repentant, fearful, horrified, overwrought?
    In one effective exit Lady Macbeth took Macbeth's hands in her's and holding them high in front urged him out.
    Should there be sounds of a storm? See II. iii, 50.

That fears a painted devil. If he do bleed,
I'll gild the faces of the grooms withal,
For it must seem their guilt.   [*Exit. Knock within*

MACBETH: Whence is that knocking?
How is't with me, when every noise appals me?
What hands are here? Ha! They pluck out mine eyes.
Will all great Neptune's ocean wash this blood   60
Clean from my hand? No, this my hand will rather
The multitudinous seas incarnadine,
Making the green one red.

Enter LADY MACBETH

LADY MACBETH: My hands are of your colour; but I shame
To wear a heart so white. [*Knock within*] I hear a knocking
At the south entry. Retire we to our chamber.
A little water clears us of this deed.
How easy is it then! Your constancy
Hath left you unattended. [*Knock within*] Hark, more knock-
  ing.
Get on your nightgown, lest occasion call us,   70
And show us to be watchers. Be not lost
So poorly in your thoughts.
MACBETH: To know my deed, 'twere best not know myself
                    [*Knock within*
Wake Duncan with thy knocking. I would thou couldst.
                    [*Exeunt*

The same

How should the Porter appear—drunken, slovenly, sinister, grotesque, devilish?

1-2   *If . . . key.* This garrulous taking the audience into his confidence and delay in opening the gate is exasperating. He now with appropriate miming parodies the Porter of hell-gate. *Porter of hell-gate,* i.e. as in the mystery plays.

2   *old,* plenty of, more than enough.

3   *Beelzebub,* one of the devils.

4-5   *Here's . . . plenty.* There was a very good harvest in 1606 which brought down the price of corn, but the allusion is common and might be a glance at the character Sordido in Ben Jonson's *Every Man Out of His Humour,* 1605.

5   *Come in time,* you are welcome, come in good time. Wilson proposed 'time-server' for 'time' to parallel the later 'equivocator' and 'tailor'. 'Time-server' would apply to a farmer who observes the seasons, and through 'server'=waiter, would provide a link with 'napkins'. *napkins,* handkerchiefs.

7   *equivocator,* one who uses words capable of a double significance in order to deceive, double talker. A reference to the Jesuit, Garnet, hanged on 3 May, 1606, for his part in the Gunpowder Plot. Garnet defended the practice of equivocation at his trial and in consequence was much discussed at the time. Garnet was also known as Farmer so that the conjunction of farmer and equivocator in this speech underlines the topical point.

12   *tailor . . . hose.* An old joke against tailors; there is also a glance at the Englishman's fondness for imitating foreign fashions. *French hose,* breeches reaching below the knee cut wide and full.

13   *goose,* tailor's iron with a play on 'goose', a bird.

16-17   *primrose . . . bonfire.* See *Hamlet,* I. iii, 50. Probably a version of *St. Matthew,* vii. 13.

17   *bonfire.* Perhaps a reminder that the remains of traitors were burnt at Tyburn.

17-18   *I . . . porter.* An appeal to the audience or to Macduff and Lennox? What significance has this—is the castle like hell, is Macbeth an equivocator or traitor?

     Is it to amuse the groundlings, to give the effect of timelessness, to reflect the depth of Macbeth's sin, to jar the audience with horror, to give relief, comic or otherwise?

SCENE THREE

Enter a PORTER. *Knocking within*

PORTER: Here's a knocking indeed! If a man were porter of hell-gate, he should have old turning the key. [*Knock within*] Knock, knock, knock. Who's there, i' th' name of Beelzebub? Here's a farmer that hanged himself on the expectation of plenty. Come in time; have napkins enow about you, here you'll sweat for't. [*Knock within*] Knock, knock. Who's there, i' th' other devil's name? Faith here's an equivocator, that could swear in both the scales against either scale, who committed treason enough for God's sake, yet could not equivocate to heaven. O come in, equivocator. [*Knock within*] Knock, knock, knock. Who's there? Faith here's an English tailor come hither, for stealing out of a French hose. Come in tailor, here you may roast your goose. [*Knock within*] Knock, knock. Never at quiet. What are you? But this place is too cold for hell. I'll devil-porter it no further. I had thought to have let in some of all professions, that go the primrose way to th' everlasting bonfire. [*Knock within*] Anon, anon! I pray you remember the porter. [*Opens the gate*

Enter MACDUFF *and* LENNOX

MACDUFF: Was it so late, friend, ere you went to bed,
That you do lie so late? 20

21   *second cock*, 3 a.m.

24   *Lechery*, lust.

27   *him*, i.e. the lustful man.

30   *equivocates . . . sleep*, i.e. tricks him into sleeping and by dreams
      while he is sleeping. Possibly a glance at what happened to
      Duncan while the grooms were stupefied. *giving . . . lie*, (*a*) making
      him lie down to sleep, (*b*) cheating him.

32   *gave . . . lie*, made you drunk.

33   *i' . . . me*, (*a*) a direct lie, (*b*) when he swallowed it.

35   *took . . . legs*, (*a*) made me stagger to the ground, (*b*) gave me a fall
      (in wrestling). *made a shift*, (*a*) contrived, (*b*) repented, i.e. shift =
      shirt, sheet. See 2 *Henry IV*, II. ii, 20–1; 2 *Henry VI*, II. iv, 107; 3
      Henry VI, III. ii, 108. *cast*, (*a*) throw (wrestling), (*b*) vomit, spew,
      (*c*) exorcise.
          Possibly these lines are a distorted reflection of Macbeth's
      wavering between desire and act. The half comic description on
      the effect of drink is horrifyingly ironic in view of what followed
      the groom's drunkenness.

37   *Our . . . him*, Ironical. See Macbeth's words, II. ii, 74.

41   *I'll . . . him*. Any sign of effort in these words?

42   *joyful trouble*. A two-edged remark. Is Macbeth showing 'trouble'?

44   *The . . . pain*. Macbeth takes refuge in a proverb.

45   *This . . . door*. Macbeth's movements should indicate tension. Does
      his nerve fail him?

46   *limited*, appointed.

47   *he . . . so*. Is this guilty confusion?

PORTER: Faith sir, we were carousing till the second cock.
and drink, sir, is a great provoker of three things.

MACDUFF: What three things does drink especially provoke?

PORTER: Marry sir, nose-painting, sleep, and urine. Lechery, sir,
it provokes, and unprovokes; it provokes the desire, but it
takes away the performance. Therefore much drink may be
said to be an equivocator with lechery; it makes him, and it
mars him; it sets him on, and it takes him off; it persuades him,
and disheartens him; makes him stand to, and not stand to; in
conclusion, equivocates him in a sleep, and, giving him the lie,
leaves him.   31

MACDUFF: I believe drink gave thee the lie last night.

PORTER: That it did sir, i' the very throat on me; but I requited
him for his lie, and I think, being too strong for him, though
he to took up my legs sometime, yet I made a shift to cast him.

MACDUFF: Is thy master stirring?
Our knocking has awaked him, here he comes.

Enter MACBETH

LENNOX: Good morrow noble sir.

MACBETH: Good morrow both.

MACDUFF: Is the King stirring, worthy Thane?

MACBETH: Not yet.

MACDUFF: He did command me to call timely on him.   40
I have almost slipped the hour.

MACBETH: I'll bring you to him.

MACDUFF: I know this is a joyful trouble to you;
But yet 'tis one.

MACBETH: The labour we delight in physics pain.
This is the door.

MACDUFF: I'll make so bold to call,
For 'tis my limited service.   [Exit

LENNOX: Goes the king hence today?

MACBETH: He does—he did appoint so.

48   *lay*, spent the night.

49   *as*, so.

52   *dire combustion*, fearful conflagration. A possible echo of Gun-
      powder Plot. See Introduction, p. 4.

53   *New . . . time*, to be produced by this wretched state of affairs.
      obscure bird, night-bird, owl.

55   *feverous*, (*a*) with sickness, (*b*) with an earthquake. See note to I. i,
      S.D. *a rough night*. A grim understatement.
           Is it just conversation about the weather, a prelude to the
      discovery about to come, or to give Macduff time to visit the
      chamber?

58   *O . . . horror*. Spoken partly off-stage and overlapping Lennox's
      words.

60   *Confusion*, destruction, ruin.

61-2 *sacreligious . . . temple*. It was held that kings were appointed by
      God as his regents and were therefore divine. Here the under-
      lying ideas are, 2 *Corinthians*, vi. 16, 'Ye are the temple of the
      living God', 1 *Samuel*, xxvi. 10, 'for who can lay his hand on
      the Lord's anointed and be guiltless?', and *St. John*, ii, 21, 'But
      he spake of the temple of his body'. *broke . . . stole*. Murder and
      theft were associated: *Job* xxiv. 14, 'The murderer . . . in the night
      is as a thief.'

66   *Gorgon*. In classical myth Medusa whose head turned to stone all
      who saw it.
           Any gestures and movements?

70-1 *death's . . . itself*. The two thoughts are linked down to 'trumpet',
      l.75, with the Day of Judgement, perhaps a reminder that the life
      to come cannot be jumped.

72   *The . . . image*, the picture of the horror of the Day of Judgement.

73   *sprites*, spirits, ghosts.

74   *countenance*, (*a*) see, (*b*) match, be in keeping with.

LENNOX: The night has been unruly. Where we lay,
Our chimneys were blown down, and as they say,
Lamentings heard i' th' air, strange screams of death,   50
And prophesying with accents terrible,
Of dire combustion, and confused events,
New hatched to the woeful time. The obscure bird
Clamoured the livelong night. Some say, the earth
Was feverous, and did shake.
MACBETH: 'Twas a rough night.
LENNOX: My young remembrance cannot parallel
A fellow to it.

Enter MACDUFF

MACDUFF: O horror, horror, horror! Tongue nor heart
Cannot conceive nor name thee.
MACBETH, LENNOX: What's the matter?
MACDUFF: Confusion now hath made his masterpiece.   60
Most sacrilegious murder hath broke ope
The Lord's anointed temple, and stole thence
The life o' th' building!
MACBETH: What is't you say—the life?
LENNOX: Mean you his Majesty?
MACDUFF: Approach the chamber, and destroy your sight
With a new Gorgon. Do not bid me speak.
See, and then speak yourselves.   [*Exeunt Macbeth and Lennox*
                      Awake, awake!
Ring the alarum-bell. Murder and treason!
Banquo and Donalbain! Malcolm awake!
Shake off this downy sleep, death's counterfeit,   70
And look on death itself! Up, up and see
The great doom's image! Malcolm! Banquo!
As from your graves rise up, and walk like sprites,
To countenance this horror!

                                    [*Bell rings*

93

75 *trumpet . . . parley*. Has the imagery of war any significance here?

84–9 *Had . . . of*. Is this hypocrisy, equivocation, irony, sincerity, self-condemning, or prophecy?

84 *chance*, mischance, calamity.

86 *serious in mortality*, of consequence in human existence.

88 *lees*, dregs. Possibly an allusion to *Psalms*, lxxv.8. See Introduction, p. 22.

89 *Is . . . of*, all that this world can boast of. *vault*, (*a*) burial vault, (*b*) cellar, (*c*) world.

91–2 *The . . . stopped*. The repetition marks Macbeth's strained agitation.

93 *O by whom?* Any gestures?

95 *badged*, marked significantly.

Act Two, Scene Three

Enter LADY MACBETH

LADY MACBETH: What's the business,
  That such a hideous trumpet calls to parley
  The sleepers of the house? Speak, speak.
MACDUFF: O gentle lady,
  'Tis not for you to hear what I can speak;
  The repetition in a woman's ear
  Would murder as it fell.

Enter BANQUO

             O Banquo, Banquo,
  Our royal master's murdered.
LADY MACBETH: Woe, alas!   80
  What, in our house?
BANQUO: Too cruel anywhere.
  Dear Duff, I prithee contradict thyself,
  And say it is not so.

Enter MACBETH *and* LENNOX

MACBETH: Had I but died an hour before this chance,
  I had lived a blessed time; for from this instant,
  There's nothing serious in mortality;
  All is but toys. Renown and grace is dead,
  The wine of life is drawn, and the mere lees
  Is left this vault to brag of.

Enter MALCOLM *and* DONALBAIN

DONALBAIN: What is amiss?
MACBETH: You are, and do not know't.   90
  The spring, the head, the fountain of your blood
  Is stopped, the very source of it is stopped.
MACDUFF: Your royal father's murdered.
MALCOLM: O, by whom?
LENNOX: Those of his chamber, as it seemed, had done't.
  Their hands and faces were all badged with blood,

97   *They . . . distracted.* With the effects of their possets.

99–   *I . . . them.* Does he?
100

101   *amazed*, frantic.

103   *expedition*, rush.

104   *pauser*, delayer.

104–   *Here . . . known.* Is this forced, unnatural, loving, sincere, agonized,
  11 or an attempt to gain sympathy or to relieve his emotions?

105   *laced*, (*a*) streaked, (*b*) embroidered, i.e. as cloth of silver laced with
       gold.

106   *breach in nature*, break through the walls of the fortress of nature.

109   *Unmannerly breeched.* The daggers that made the breach in nature
       are unnaturally covered with breeches of blood.

111   *Help . . . ho!* Is Lady Macbeth overwrought by the reconstruction
       of the scene, or is her faint not real, but an astute diversion?

113   *That . . . ours*, who have the greatest claim to make our voices
       heard. *argument*, subject-matter.

115   *hid . . . auger-hole*, i.e. secret well-concealed. A hint at witchcraft.
       Witches 'can go in and out at awger holes' (Scot.)

118   *Upon . . . motion*, is ready to show itself.

122   *scruples*, suspicions, doubts. *shake*, disturb.

So were their daggers, which unwiped we found
Upon their pillows. They stared, and were distracted,
No man's life was to be trusted with them.

MACBETH: O yet I do repent me of my fury,
That I did kill them.

MACDUFF: Wherefore did you so?   100

MACBETH: Who can be wise, amazed, temperate and furious,
Loyal and neutral, in a moment? No man.
The expedition of my violent love
Outrun the pauser, reason. Here lay Duncan,
His silver skin laced with his golden blood,
And his gashed stabs looked like a breach in nature
For ruin's wasteful entrance; there the murderers,
Steeped in the colours of their trade, their daggers
Unmannerly breeched with gore. Who could refrain,
That had a heart to love, and in that heart   110
Courage to make's love known?

LADY MACBETH: Help me hence, ho! [*Faints*

MACDUFF: Look to the lady.

MALCOLM: [*Aside to Donalbain*] Why do we hold our tongues,
That most may claim this argument for ours?

DONALBAIN: [*Aside to Malcolm*] What should be spoken here,
    where our fate,
Hid in an auger-hole, may rush and seize us?
Let's away;
Our tears are not yet brewed.

MALCOLM: [*Aside to Donalbain*] Nor our strong sorrow
Upon the foot of motion.

BANQUO: Look to the lady.
                    [*Lady Macbeth is carried out*

And when we have our naked frailties hid,
That suffer in exposure, let us meet,   120
And question this most bloody piece of work,
To know it further. Fears and scruples shake us.

123– *In . . . malice.* Banquo takes an oath in which the others join. Any
  5 gesture or movement?

     Banquo's phrases are reminiscent of the Bond of Association
  formed by Scottish nobles to support and protect James in 1599:
  'In the name of the great God . . . to maintain and defend . . . his
  . . . right . . . against all other pretenders . . .'.

124 *undivulged pretence,* hidden plot.

     Are the rhymes 'hand', 'stand'; 'thence', 'pretence' of any
  significance?

126 *put . . . readiness,* (*a*) dress ourselves, (*b*) prepare for action.

129 *office,* action.

133– *the . . . bloody.* A grim quibble.
  34
133 *near in blood,* closer related.

137 *dainty,* particular, over-nice.

138 *warrant,* honourable reason.

Outside the castle

Do Ross and the Old Man meet or are they continuing a conversation?

1 *Threescore and ten.* A biblical echo implying extreme age and the
  integrity of the speaker.

3 *sore,* bitter, fearful.

4 *trifled former knowings,* made previous experiences seem mere
  trifles.

5 *heavens,* (*a*) Heaven, (*b*) sky, clouds, (*c*) stage canopy. *act,*
  (*a*) deed, (*b*) stage performance.

In the great hand of God I stand, and thence
Against the undivulged pretence I fight
Of treasonous malice.
MACDUFF: And so do I.
ALL: So all.
MACBETH: Let's briefly put on manly readiness,
And meet i' th' hall together.
ALL: Well contented.
                [Exeunt all but Malcolm and Donalbain
MALCOLM: What will you do? Let's not consort with them.
To show an unfelt sorrow is an office
Which the false man does easy. I'll to England.   130
DONALBAIN: To Ireland I. Our separated fortune
Shall keep us both the safer. Where we are,
There's daggers in men's smiles; the near in blood,
The nearer bloody.
MALCOLM: This murderous shaft that's shot
Hath not yet lighted, and our safest way
Is to avoid the aim. Therefore to horse,
And let us not be dainty of leave-taking,
But shift away. There's warrant in that theft
Which steals itself, when there's no mercy left.   *[Exeunt*

SCENE FOUR

Enter ROSS *and an* OLD MAN

OLD MAN: Threescore and ten I can remember well,
Withing the volume of which time I have seen
Hours dreadful, and things strange; but this sore night
Hath trifled former knowings.
ROSS: Ha, good father,
Thou seest the heavens, as troubled with man's act,

6   *stage*, (*a*) world, (*b*) scene.

7   *travelling*, (*a*) journeying, (*b*) labouring, struggling. *lamp*, sun.

8   *predominance*, overmastering power, influence of the stars.

9   *That . . . entomb.* See *St. Matthew*, xxvii. 45; *St. Luke*, xxiii. 44–5.

12   *towering*, circling higher. *pride of place*, highest-point of her soaring.

15   *minions*, choicest.

24   *pretend*, intend, aim at. *suborned*, bribed.

27   '*Gainst nature still.* The conversation stresses the unnaturalness of events, the breaking down of order in nature.

28–9 *Thriftless . . . means.* Walker notes that this applies to Macbeth as well as to Malcolm and Donalbain.

28   *ravin up*, swallow, devour.

29   *means*, support, i.e. Duncan.

Threatens his bloody stage: by th' clock 'tis day,
And yet dark night strangles the travelling lamp.
Is't night's predominance, or the day's shame,
That darkness does the face of earth entomb,
When living light should kiss it?
OLD MAN: 'Tis unnatural,   10
Even like the deed that's done. On Tuesday last,
A falcon towering in her pride of place
Was by a mousing owl hawked at, and killed.
ROSS: And Duncan's horses—a thing most strange and certain—
Beauteous and swift, the minions of their race,
Turned wild in nature, broke their stalls, flung out,
Contending 'gainst obedience, as they would make
War with mankind.
OLD MAN: 'Tis said they eat each other.
ROSS: They did so, to th' amazement of mine eyes
That looked upon't. Here comes the good Macduff.   20

Enter MACDUFF

How goes the world sir, now?
MACDUFF: Why, see you not?
ROSS: Is't known who did this more than bloody deed?
MACDUFF: Those that Macbeth hath slain.
ROSS: Alas the day,
What good could they pretend?
MACDUFF: They were suborned.
Malcolm and Donalbain, the King's two sons,
Are stolen away and fled, which puts upon them
Suspicion of the deed.
ROSS: 'Gainst nature still.
Thriftless ambition, that will ravin up
Thine own life's means! Then 'tis most like
The sovereignty will fall upon Macbeth.   30

31   *named*, elected.

34–5   *sacred . . . bones*. Emphasis on Duncan's divine nature.

37   *Well . . . well*, ironical repetition of Ross's 'well' (Muir).

40   *benison*, blessing.

40–1   *and . . . foes*. Is this an innocent wish or a contemptuous fling at Ross as a time-server?

     Is the purpose of this scene—to sum up events that would hinder the movement of the play, to give a chorus comment, to set the murder in a perspective of time and being?

MACDUFF: He is already named, and gone to Scone
  To be invested.
ROSS: Where is Duncan's body?
MACDUFF: Carried to Colme-kill,
  The sacred storehouse of his predecessors,
  And guardian of their bones.
ROSS: Will you to Scone?
MACDUFF: No cousin, I'll to Fife.
ROSS: Well, I will thither.
MACDUFF: Well, may you see things well done there. Adieu.
  Lest our old robes sit easier than our new!
ROSS: Farewell father.
OLD MAN: God's benison go with you, and with those   40
  That would make good of bad, and friends of foes.

                                        [*Exeunt*

The palace at Forres

Is Banquo meditating, furtive, alarmed, bewildered? Is he talking confidentially to the audience, speaking his thoughts aloud, addressing, say, an empty throne or some emblem of royalty?

3   *play'dst*, plotted.

4   *stand*, remain.

5   *root*. Paul notes that in a genealogical tree of James I's ancestors in Leslie's *De Origine* Banquo's name is placed at the root of the stem.

7   *shine*, throw the light of truth.

10   *But . . . more*. Is this because he hears the sennet, or because he brushes aside his own thoughts for fear they lead him into evil? Is Banquo an accessory to the murder?

S.D.   *Sennet*. A set of notes played on a trumpet or cornet to announce a ceremonial entry.

13   *all-thing*, altogether, wholly.

14   *solemn*, formal, in full state.

16–18 *my . . . knit*. A formal, correct reply.

ACT THREE

SCENE ONE

Enter BANQUO

BANQUO: Thou hast it now, King, Cawdor, Glamis, all,
   As the weird women promised, and I fear
   Thou play'dst most foully for't; yet it was said
   It should not stand in thy posterity,
   But that myself should be the root and father
   Of many kings. If there come truth from them,
   As upon thee Macbeth, their speeches shine,
   Why by the verities on thee made good
   May they not be my oracles as well,
   And set me up in hope? But hush, no more.   10

Sennet sounded. Enter MACBETH *as King,* LADY MACBETH
   as Queen, LENNOX, ROSS, LORDS, LADIES, *and* ATTEN-
   DANTS

MACBETH: Here's our chief guest.
LADY MACBETH: If he had been forgotten,
   It had been as a gap in our great feast,
   And all-thing unbecoming.
MACBETH: Tonight we hold a solemn supper sir,
   And I'll request your presence.
BANQUO: Let your Highness
   Command upon me, to the which my duties
   Are with a most indissoluble tie
   For ever knit.
MACBETH: Ride you this afternoon?
BANQUO: Ay, my good lord.   20

Macbeth

22 *still*, always. *grave*, authoritative. *prosperous*, successful.

26 *better*, faster than usual.

28 *twain*, two.

33 *strange invention*, i.e. stories of Macbeth's guilt.
34 *cause*, matters.
35 *Hie*, hurry.

37 *our . . . upon's.* Has Banquo been anxious to go throughout this conversation, is he not anxious for an understanding with Macbeth, is he embarrassed by Macbeth's pressing courtesy and inquiries? In view of the two soliloquies, III. i, 1–10 and 48–72, are the two fencing with each other?

48–9 *To . . . thus*, to be king as I am is worth nothing, but to be secure on my throne is everything.
48–54 *To . . . safety.* Does Macbeth suspect that Banquo will plot against him?
50 *Stick deep*, i.e. like daggers.
50–1 *his . . . feared*, his natural, king-like dignity inspires awe. Is this flattery intended for James I, or a natural train of thought?

MACBETH: We should have else desired your good advice,
  Which still hath been both grave and prosperous,
  In this day's council; but we'll take tomorrow.
  Is't far you ride?
BANQUO: As far, my lord, as will fill up the time
  'Twixt this and supper. Go not my horse the better,
  I must become a borrower of the night
  For a dark hour or twain.
MACBETH: Fail not our feast.
BANQUO: My lord, I will not.
MACBETH: We hear our bloody cousins are bestowed   30
  In England and in Ireland, not confessing
  Their cruel parricide, filling their hearers
  With strange invention. But of that tomorrow,
  When therewithal we shall have cause of state
  Craving us jointly. Hie you to horse. Adieu,
  Till you return at night. Goes Fleance with you?
BANQUO: Ay my good lord; our time does call upon's.
MACBETH: I wish your horses swift, and sure of foot;
  And so I do commend you to their backs.
  Farewell.   [*Exit Banquo*   40
  Let every man be master of his time
  Till seven at night; to make society
  The sweeter welcome, we will keep ourself
  Till supper-time alone. While then, God be with you!
                    [*Exeunt all but Macbeth and an Attendant*
  Sirrah, a word with you. Attend those men
  Our pleasure?
ATTENDANT: They are, my lord, without the palace gate.
MACBETH: Bring them before us.   [*Exit Attendant*
                    To be thus is nothing,
  But to be safely thus. Our fears in Banquo
  Stick deep, and in his royalty of nature   50
  Reigns that which would be feared. 'Tis much he dares,

52   *temper*, quality.

55-7   *under . . . Cæsar.* A man's guardian spirit, it was believed, could
        be over-awed and influenced by the stronger spirit of another
        man. See *Antony and Cleopatra*, II. iii, 20–1,
                'But, near him [Cæsar], thy angel
                Becomes afeard, as being o'erpowered'.

61-2   *fruitless . . . sceptre.* Macbeth has no son, a negation of all that a
        king stood for.
63   *unlineal*, not of my descendants.
64   *No . . . succeeding.* Not so prophesied by the witches though so
        interpreted by Macbeth. See Appendix, p. 207.
65   *filed*, defiled.
67   *rancours*, bitterness. *Put . . . peace.* See *Psalms* xi. 7, 'Upon the wicked
        he shall rain snares, fire and brimstone, storm and tempest; this
        shall be their portion to drink.' Others see a reference to the
        communion chalice. See I. vii, 11.
68   *eternal jewel*, immortal soul.
69   *common . . . man.* Satan.
71-2   *come . . . utterance.* Is Macbeth challenging fate, or calling on Fate
        to help him?
71   *list*, tournament field.
72   *to th' utterance*, to the death.
             Is Macbeth aggrieved, indignant, angry, remorseful, bitter, or
        committed to evil?
S.D.   *two Murderers.* Hotson suggests that stage murderers wore masks.
             An ironically apt entry following Macbeth's invocation.

78   *under fortune*, in wretchedness below your true worth.

80   *passed . . . you*, spent the time in proving to you.
81   *borne in hand*, tricked, deceived. *crossed*, thwarted. *instruments*,
        means.

And to that dauntless temper of his mind,
He hath a wisdom that doth guide his valour
To act in safety. There is none but he
Whose being I do fear; and under him
My Genius is rebuked, as it is said
Mark Antony's was by Cæsar. He chid the sisters,
When first they put the name of king upon me,
And bade them speak to him. Then, prophet-like,
They hailed him father to a line of kings.   60
Upon my head they placed a fruitless crown,
And put a barren sceptre in my gripe,
Thence to be wrenched with an unlineal hand,
No son of mine succeeding. If't be so,
For Banquo's issue have I filed my mind,
For them the gracious Duncan have I murdered,
Put rancours in the vessel of my peace
Only for them, and mine eternal jewel
Given to the common enemy of man,
To make them kings, the seed of Banquo kings.   70
Rather than so, come fate, into the list,
And champion me to th' utterance. Who's there?

Enter SERVANT, *with two* MURDERERS

Now go to the door, and stay there till we call.

[*Exit Servant*

Was it not yesterday we spoke together?
FIRST MURDERER: It was, so please your Highness.
MACBETH: Well then, now
Have you considered of my speeches? Know
That it was he in the times past which held you
So under fortune, which you thought had been
Our innocent self. This I made good to you
In our last conference, passed in probation with you,   80
How you were borne in hand, how crossed; the instruments.

82–4   *that . . . Banquo*, that even to a half-wit or mental defective it would be clear that these things were done by Banquo.

83   *half a soul*, a half-wit. *notion*, mind.

84   *You . . . us.* Is he suspicious, sceptical, indifferent, or dim-witted?

88–9   *Are . . . man?* i.e. are you so piously brought up as to love your enemies? See *St. Matthew*, v. 44. Macbeth is heavily sarcastic.

    Muir (Arden) notes in the scenes relating to the murder of Banquo there seem to be several echoes from verses in the same chapter . . . implying that Banquo is persecuted for righteousness' sake.

91   *We are men*, i.e. and therefore ready for revenge.

92   *Ay . . . men.* Macbeth knows the effectiveness of an appeal to manhood. See I. vii, 46–51.

93–   *As . . . alike.* James kept a large establishment for the obtaining
101 and training of dogs in which he was deeply interested (see Paul). Apart from a possible appeal to James, these lines are, perhaps prompted by a passage in Erasmus' *Colloquia*, ('Philodoxus') then used in schools, depicting the theme of order at a low level.

94   *Shoughs*, shaggy dogs. *water-rugs*, rough water-dogs. *clept*, called.

95   *valued file*, list in which the qualities of each kind are set down.

96   *subtle*, clever.

97   *housekeeper*, watchdog.

99   *closed*, enclosed.

100   *Particular addition*, special title. *from*, apart from.

102   *file*, (*a*) list, (*b*) rank (of soldiers).

105   *takes . . . off*, removes, kills.

107   *in his life*, as long as he is alive.

Who wrought with them; and all things else that might
To half a soul and to a notion crazed
Say 'Thus did Banquo.'

FIRST MURDERER: You made it known to us.

MACBETH: I did so; and went further, which is now
Our point of second meeting. Do you find
Your patience so predominant in your nature,
That you can let this go? Are you so gospelled
To pray for this good man, and for his issue,
Whose heavy hand hath bowed you to the grave,   90
And beggared yours for ever?

FIRST MURDERER: We are men, my liege.

MACBETH: Ay, in the catalogue ye go for men,
As hounds, and greyhounds, mongrels, spaniels, curs,
Shoughs, water-rugs, and demi-wolves are clept
All by the name of dogs; the valued file
Distinguishes the swift, the slow, the subtle,
The housekeeper, the hunter, every one
According to the gift which bounteous nature
Hath in him closed, whereby he does receive
Particular addition, from the bill   100
That writes them all alike; and so of men.
Now if you have a station in the file,
Not i' th' worst rank of manhood, say't,
And I will put that business in your bosoms,
Whose execution takes your enemy off,
Grapples you to the heart and love of us,
Who wear our health but sickly in his life,
Which in his death were perfect.

SECOND MURDERER: I am one, my liege,
Whom the vile blows and buffets of the world
Have so incensed, that I am reckless what   110
I do to spite the world.

FIRST MURDERER: And I another

112   *tugged*, dragged this way and that.

114–15*Both . . . enemy.* Any movement to ensure secrecy?

116   *bloody distance*, (*a*) murderous enmity, (*b*) deadly striking distance
        between fencers.
117–   *thrusts . . . life*, threatens most narrowly my very life, or, is like a
    18 dagger threatening my very life. See ll. 49–50 ' Our fears . . . Stick
        deep'. Muir takes 'near'st of life' as 'vital parts'.
120   *avouch*, justify.

122   *but*, but must.

        Macbeth cuts the First Murderer short presumably because
        time is short.

130   *the . . . time.* A much debated phrase. (*a*) the exact time most
        suitable for the murder, (*b*) the Third Murderer, (*c*) spy o' th'
        =spial(l)=watching, i.e. the precise watching time.
132   *something*, some distance. *thought*, bearing in mind.
133   *clearness*, clean job.
134   *rubs*, roughnesses. *botches*, clumsy bunglings.
136   *material*, important.
136–8   *absence . . . hour.* Does Macbeth shrink from blunt words, or do
        the later words recall the destiny that hangs on the killing of
        Fleance?
139   *anon*, soon.

So weary with disasters, tugged with fortune,
That I would set my life on any chance,
To mend it, or be rid on't.

MACBETH: Both of you
  Know Banquo was your enemy.

BOTH MURDERERS: True my lord.

MACBETH: So is he mine; and in such bloody distance
  That every minute of his being thrusts
  Against my near'st of life; and though I could
  With barefaced power sweep him from my sight,
  And bid my will avouch it, yet I must not,   120
  For certain friends that are both his and mine,
  Whose loves I may not drop, but wail his fall
  Who I myself struck down. And thence it is,
  That I to your assistance do make love,
  Masking the business from the common eye
  For sundry weighty reasons.

SECOND MURDERER: We shall, my lord,
  Perform what you command us.

FIRST MURDERER: Though our lives—

MACBETH: Your spirits shine through you. Within this hour at
    most,
  I will advise you where to plant yourselves,
  Acquaint you with the perfect spy o' th' time,   130
  The moment on't, for't must be done tonight,
  And something from the palace; always thought
  That I require a clearness: and with him—
  To leave no rubs nor botches in the work—
  Fleance his son, that keeps him company,
  Whose absence is no less material to me
  Than is his father's, must embrace the fate
  Of that dark hour. Resolve yourselves apart,
  I'll come to you anon.

BOTH MURDERERS: We are resolved, my lord.

141–2 Is the couplet gloating, grim, resolute, or self-congratulatory?

The palace at Forres

1–2 *Is . . . tonight.* Is Lady Macbeth suspicious of Macbeth's intentions? Is this a reminder to the audience?

4 *Nought's . . . spent,* nothing has been gained, all has been lost.

5 *content,* peace of mind.

7 *doubtful,* full of fear.

Is Lady Macbeth beginning to break down, is she here a mouth-piece for Macbeth's thoughts, or is she introducing the mood of the aftermath emphatically in rhyme?

Any movement or gesture?

8 *alone.* Is this melancholy, despair, suspicion, or self-torture?

10 *Using,* pursuing, accompanying.

12 *without regard,* ignored. *what's . . . done.* See I. vii, 1; V. i, 60–1.

13 *scorched,* slashed, gashed. Theobald's emendation 'scotch'd' is preferred by some editors. Both words are of the same origin. Macbeth is almost rapt as he speaks ignoring his wife.

14–15 *whilst . . . tooth,* while our half-hearted attempt (to kill her) is threatened by the same venom as before.

16 *But . . . suffer.* Folio prints this as two lines, and editors suspect cuts in the text. *frame . . . disjoint,* the universe fall to pieces. *both the worlds,* i.e. heaven and earth.

Macbeth would prefer disorder and chaos in the universe to undergoing these afflictions himself. Is this a turning point for him?

18–19 *terrible . . . nightly.* Of re-enacting the murder, of being murdered, or of being punished (racked?) for the treasonable murder?

19 *shake,* i.e. with terror.

19–20 *Better . . . peace.* See ll. 6–7.

20 *to peace,* i.e. to pacify our desires have sent to the peace of death. See Introduction, p. 29.

21 *on . . . lie,* i.e. as on the rack.

MACBETH: I'll call upon you straight; abide within.   140
[Exeunt Murderers

It is concluded. Banquo, thy soul's flight,
If it find heaven, must find it out tonight.   *[Exit*

SCENE TWO

Enter LADY MACBETH *and a* SERVANT

LADY MACBETH: Is Banquo gone from Court?
SERVANT: Ay madam, but returns again tonight.
LADY MACBETH: Say to the King, I would attend his leisure
For a few words.
SERVANT: Madam I will.   *[Exit*
LADY MACBETH: Nought's had, all's spent,
Where our desire is got without content.
'Tis safer to be that which we destroy,
Than by destruction dwell in doubtful joy.

Enter MACBETH

How now my lord? Why do you keep alone,
Of sorriest fancies your companions making,
Using those thoughts which should indeed have died   10
With them they think on? Things without all remedy
Should be without regard: what's done is done.
MACBETH: We have scorched the snake, not killed it:
She'll close, and be herself, whilst our poor malice
Remains in danger of her former tooth.
But let the frame of things disjoint, both the worlds suffer,
Ere we will eat our meal in fear, and sleep
In the affliction of these terrible dreams
That shake us nightly. Better be with the dead,
Whom we, to gain our peace, have sent to peace,   20
Than on the torture of the mind to lie

22 *ecstasy*, fear, frenzy, emotion.

22–6 *Duncan . . . further*. Macbeth envies his victim although he has just arranged for Banquo to 'sleep well'—a miscalculation!

25 *levy*, army.

27 *Gentle*, noble, *sleek o'er*, smooth.

30 *Let . . . Banquo*, you in turn remember Banquo particularly, have Banquo very much in mind.

31 *Present him eminence*, assign to him the highest rank (Muir), show him honour.

32–3 *Unsafe . . . streams*, i.e. we are unsafe at present, so that we must wash over our honours with streams of flattery.

34 *vizards*, masks.

36 *full . . . mind*, (*a*) pricking of conscience, (*b*) jealousy of Banquo, (*c*) tortures of fear. Some see a reference to the belief that scorpions grew inside men who smelled the herb basil. It is more likely to be an echo of *Revelation*, ix. 3–5: 'came out of the smoke locusts upon the earth: and unto them was given power, as the scorpions of the earth have power. And it was commanded them that should not hurt the grass . . . but only those men which have not the seal of God in their foreheads. And to them it was given that they should not kill them, but that they should be vexed five months; and their pain was as the pain . . . of a scorpion, when he striketh a man.'

There is also a similarity of thought between ll. 19–25 and the next verse: 'And in those days shall men seek death, and shall not find it; and shall desire to die, and death shall flee from them and although punishment followed men did not repent of their murders, nor of their sorceries, nor of their fornications, nor of their thefts.'

38 *nature's . . . eterne*, (*a*) that as men they will die, or (*b*) that not being immortal they can be killed. *copy*, (*a*) pattern, (*b*) copyhold. *eterne*, eternal.

39 *There's*, in that there's.

40 *be thou jocund*. See l. 28.

41 *cloistered*, (*a*) among cloisters, (*b*) dim. *black*, (*a*) of the night, (*b*) evil.

42 *shard-borne*, flying on scaly wings. Some prefer 'shard-born', i.e. dung-born, according to a common Elizabethan belief.

42–4 *beetle . . . note*. Imagery Shakespeare elsewhere associates with death.

43 *yawning peal*, curfew.

In restless ecstasy. Duncan is in his grave,
After life's fitful fever he sleeps well,
Treason has done his worst: nor steel, nor poison,
Malice domestic, foreign levy, nothing,
Can touch him further.

LADY MACBETH: Come on.
Gentle my lord, sleek o'er your rugged looks,
Be bright and jovial among your guests tonight.

MACBETH: So shall I, love, and so I pray be you.
Let your remembrance apply to Banquo,   30
Present him eminence both with eye and tongue—
Unsafe the while that we
Must lave our honours in these flattering streams,
And make our faces vizards to our hearts,
Disguising what they are.

LADY MACBETH: You must leave this.

MACBETH: O full of scorpions is my mind, dear wife.
Thou know'st that Banquo, and his Fleance, lives.

LADY MACBETH: But in them nature's copy's not eterne.

MACBETH: There's comfort yet, they are assailable;
Then be thou jocund. Ere the bat hath flown   40
His cloistered flight, ere to black Hecate's summons
The shard-borne beetle with his drowsy hums
Hath rung night's yawning peal, there shall be done

44   *note*, notoriety.

45   *dearest chuck*. A touch of playful tenderness that grates in its context. Any movement or gesture?

46–55 *Come . . . ill*. This invocation parallels that of Lady Macbeth, I. v,
38–52; Macbeth commits himself utterly to evil. Is Lady Macbeth
alarmed or approving?

46   *seeling*, dark-bringing. To 'seel' was to sew together the eyelids of
a hawk until it was trained to wear a hood.

47   *Scarf . . . day*, i.e. (*a*) to prevent pity, (*b*) to maintain darkness for
evil deeds.

49   *great bond*. Variously explained: (*a*) law of nature, or the great chain
of being, (*b*) lease on nature of the lives of Banquo and Fleance,
(*c*) the prophecy of the Weird Sisters to Banquo, (*d*) christian
conscience.

50   *crow*, i.e. rook.

51   *rooky*, i.e. with a rookery. Many emendations and interpretations
of this word have been put forward.

52–5 *Good . . . ill*. The rhymes mark the onset of evil, and sum up as in
a proverb Macbeth's fallacious justification for a further murder.

56   *So . . . me*. Macbeth now takes the lead.

A park near the palace

How should the Murderers enter—from different doors, together, at
intervals, with drawn weapons, boldly, stealthily?

S.D.   *three Murderers*. The Third Murderer has roused curiosity. Is he
Macbeth, a supernatural agent, the 'perfect spy o' th' time', or
Macbeth's spirit?

2   *He . . . mistrust*, we need not be suspicious of him.

3   *offices*, duties.

4   *To . . . just*, exactly as directed by Macbeth.

5–7   *The . . . inn*. What significance have these lines—to note the beauty
of the evening or the oncoming of darkness; to symbolize
Banquo's approach to the inn of death, or the ending of his life;
or to curse the lingering day, with an evil chuckle at the
fearful traveller?

6   *lated*, belated. *apace*, quickly.

7   *timely*, in time.

A deed of dreadful note.

LADY MACBETH: What's to be done?

MACBETH: Be innocent of the knowledge, dearest chuck,
   Till thou applaud the deed. Come seeling night,
   Scarf up the tender eye of pitiful day,
   And with thy bloody and invisible hand
   Cancel and tear to pieces that great bond
   Which keeps me pale. Light thickens, and the crow   50
   Makes wing to th' rooky wood.
   Good things of day begin to droop and drowse,
   Whiles night's black agents to their preys do rouse.
   Thou marvell'st at my words; but hold thee still,
   Things bad begun make strong themselves by ill.
   So prithee go with me.   [*Exeunt*

SCENE THREE

Enter three MURDERERS

FIRST MURDERER: But who did bid thee join with us?

THIRD MURDERER: Macbeth.

SECOND MURDERER: He needs not our mistrust, since he delivers
   Our offices, and what we have to do,
   To the direction just.

FIRST MURDERER: Then stand with us.
   The west yet glimmers with some streaks of day.
   Now spurs the lated traveller apace
   To gain the timely inn, and near approaches

9–10 *The . . . expectation*, all the others that are in the list of expected guests.

11 *His . . . about*, i.e. are being taken round to the stables by grooms. Any sound of hoofs or footsteps?

S.D. *Enter . . . torch*. Fleance is carrying the torch before his father. How old should he be? Does he attempt to fight? What is done with Banquo's body?

The palace

This is the hour of triumph for Macbeth and Lady Macbeth. The banquet should be presented with full ceremony.

Stage properties are required—dining table, benches or stools, chairs of state, thrones. The seating arrangements need careful consideration see l. 10. Should Macbeth stand or sit as he speaks?

1 *degrees*, rank, order of precedence.

1–2 *At . . . last*, from the beginning to the end, all through.

The subject of our watch.

THIRD MURDERER: Hark! I hear horses.

BANQUO: [*Within*] Give us a light there, ho!

SECOND MURDERER: Then 'tis he. The rest
  That are within the note of expectation   10
  Already are i' th' Court.

FIRST MURDERER: His horses go about.

THIRD MURDERER: Almost a mile; but he does usually,
  So all men do, from hence to th' palace gate
  Make it their walk.

          Enter BANQUO, *and* FLEANCE *with a torch*

SECOND MURDERER: A light, a light!

THIRD MURDERER: 'Tis he.

FIRST MURDERER: Stand to't.

BANQUO: It will be rain tonight.

FIRST MURDERER: Let it come down.

                                [*They assault Banquo*

BANQUO: O treachery! Fly good Fleance, fly, fly, fly!
  Thou mayst revenge. O slave!   [*Dies. Fleance escapes*

THIRD MURDERER: Who did strike out the light?

FIRST MURDERER: Was't not the way?

THIRD MURDERER: There's but one down; the son is fled.

SECOND MURDERER: We have lost   20
  Best half of our affair.

FIRST MURDERER: Well let's away, and say how much is done.

                                          [*Exeunt*

SCENE FOUR

A banquet prepared. Enter MACBETH, LADY MACBETH, ROSS,
LENNOX, LORDS, *and* ATTENDANTS

MACBETH: You know your own degrees, sit down. At first
  And last the hearty welcome.

3   *society*, the company.

5   *keeps her state*, remains in her chair of state. *state*, chair or throne with a canopy.

6   *require*, request.

8   *For . . . welcome*, from my heart I offer them a welcome.

Where should the murderer place himself?

9   *See . . . thanks*. Any actions—a toast, a standing up, or a bowing?

10   *here . . . midst*. Does Macbeth sit down or does he indicate his seat?

11   *large*, free, relaxed.

12–21   *There's . . . again*. What are the guests doing during this conversation? What is Lady Macbeth doing?

Why does the murderer appear during the banquet—to emphasize the contrast between superficial royal splendour and treacherous murder, to concentrate the intense clash of emotion and imagination in Macbeth, to intensify and concentrate the impact of the appearance of Banquo's ghost?

14   *Tis . . . within*, it is better that his blood should be on your face than in his veins.

19   *nonpareil*, without equal.

21   *fit*, mood, crisis. *perfect*. Perhaps pronounced 'perfit' and quibbling with 'fit'. See III. i, 108.

22   *Whole*, (*a*) in good health, (*b*) intact, unbroken. *founded*, immovable, secure.

23   *broad and general*, free and universal. *casing*, surrounding.

24   *cribbed*, shut in a stall.

25   *saucy*, sharp, insistent, insolent.

25–9   *But . . . lies*. The emphasis is on 'safe', and Macbeth's feeling of security. See III. v, 32–3.

27   *trenched*, deeply cut.

28   *a . . . nature*, would kill a man.

29   *worm*, serpent.

LORDS: Thanks to your Majesty.

MACBETH: Ourself will mingle with society,
And play the humble host.
Our hostess keeps her state, but in best time
We will require her welcome.

LADY MACBETH: Pronounce it for me sir, to all our friends,
For my heart speaks they are welcome.
Enter first MURDERER *to the door*

MACBETH: See, they encounter thee with their hearts' thanks.
Both sides are even, here I'll sit i' th' midst.   10
Be large in mirth, anon we'll drink a measure
The table round. [*Goes to the door*] There's blood upon thy
face.

MURDERER: 'Tis Banquo's then.

MACBETH: 'Tis better thee without than he within.
Is he dispatched?

MURDERER: My lord, his throat is cut; that I did for him.

MACBETH: Thou art the best o' th' cut-throats, yet he's good
That did the like for Fleance. If thou didst it,
Thou art the nonpareil.

MURDERER: Most royal sir,
Fleance is 'scaped.   20

MACBETH: Then comes my fit again. I had else been perfect.
Whole as the marble, founded as the rock,
As broad and general as the casing air;
But now I am cabined, cribbed, confined, bound in
To saucy doubts and fears. But Banquo's safe?

MURDERER: Ay my good lord: safe in a ditch he bides,
With twenty trenched gashes on his head,
The least a death to nature.

MACBETH: Thanks for that.
There the grown serpent lies; the worm that's fled
Hath nature that in time will venom breed,   30
No teeth for th' present. Get thee gone, tomorrow

123

32   *ourselves,* each other.

33   *sold,* i.e. a meal for which one pays.

34   *vouched,* commended by courtesies.

35   *To feed,* mere eating.

36–7 *From . . . it,* away from home courteous entertainment adds, like
      sauce, a pleasure to the food; a gathering of people would be cold
      and empty without it.

36   *ceremony,* courtesies.

37   *remembrancer.* See III. ii, 30.

S.D.   How should the ghost enter—normally, through a trap-door,
      slowly, or masked by others—presuming someone does enter?

40   *our country's honour,* the chief nobility of Scotland, or, perhaps
      Banquo. *roofed,* under our roof.

41–3 *Were . . . mischance.* Defiant irony.

41   *graced,* (*a*) gracious, (*b*) received into heavenly grace.

42   *challenge,* blame, with perhaps a glance at the meaning 'summon
      to a dual'.

43   *mischance,* (*a*) bad luck, (*b*) disaster.

48   *What . . . Highness?* Should Macbeth recoil, cover his face, retreat
      from the seat, point fearfully? Lavater cited two stories in which
      murderers out of fear imagined that the ghost of their victim
      appeared to them, once as the murderer was at supper.

49   *done this,* (*a*) killed Banquo, (*b*) played this trick upon me.

50   *Thou . . . it,* i.e. in the sense that he did not actually stab Banquo.

50–1 *never . . . me,* i.e. the Ghost is nodding accusingly.

53–8 *Sit . . . not.* Is Lady Macbeth standing or sitting?

We'll hear ourselves again.   [*Exit murderer*

LADY MACBETH: My royal lord,
  You do not give the cheer. The feast is sold
  That is not often vouched, while 'tis a-making,
  'Tis given with welcome. To feed were best at home;
  From thence the sauce to meat is ceremony,
  Meeting were bare without it.

MACBETH: Sweet remembrancer!
  Now, good digestion wait on appetite,
  And health on both.

LENNOX: May't please your Highness sit.
                 [*The Ghost of Banquo enters, and sits in*
                   Macbeth's seat.

MACBETH: Here had we now our country's honour roofed, 40
  Were the graced person of our Banquo present;
  Who may I rather challenge for unkindness,
  Than pity for mischance.

ROSS: His absence sir,
  Lays blame upon his promise. Please't your Highness
  To grace us with your royal company.

MACBETH: The table's full.

LENNOX: Here is a place reserved, sir.

MACBETH: Where?

LENNOX: Here my good lord. What is't that moves your
  Highness?

MACBETH: Which of you have done this?

LORDS: What, my good lord?

MACBETH: Thou canst not say I did it; never shake   50
  Thy gory locks at me.

ROSS: Gentlemen rise, his Highness is not well.

LADY MACBETH: Sit worthy friends. My lord is often thus,
  And hath been from his youth. Pray you keep seat,
  The fit is momentary, upon a thought
  He will again be well. If much you note him,

57 *offend*, annoy. *extend his passion*, prolong his agitation or suffering.

59–60 *that . . . devil*. Is the visitant—a ghost, an illusion of Macbeth's disordered mind, or the creation of a demon?

60 *O proper stuff*, a fine bit of nonsense.

61 *painting*, visible representation.

62 *air-drawn*, (*a*) pictured in air, (*b*) drawn through the air.

63 *flaws*, outbursts of feeling.

64 *to*, by comparison with.

65–6 *woman's . . . grandam*, i.e. an old wives' tale of superstitious happenings.

    Is Lady Macbeth angry, frightened, scornful, resourceful, whispering, impatient?

67 *Why . . . faces*. Is Macbeth's face working, is he trying to speak, screwing up his eyes, or weeping and turning away from the ghost?

    Is the ghost still or moving during these speeches?

71 *charnel-houses*, vaults, tombs.

71–3 *If . . . kites*, (*a*) If bodies return from the grave our tombs will be like the stomachs of kites which disgorge their food, (*b*) if bodies return from the grave, we shall have to leave them unburied to be eaten by kites which will thus become their monuments. The kite was known to disgorge portions of its food.

73 *folly*, madness.

76 *humane*, (*a*) human, (*b*) merciful. *purged . . . weal*, cleansed the kingdom and made it peaceful.

81 *twenty mortal murders*, twenty wounds each one mortal. See ll. 26–7.

    Macbeth is oblivious of the company. How should his actions show this?

83–4 *My . . . you*. Lady Macbeth previously talking privately now changes tactics and reminds Macbeth of his duty as host fearing lest he shall confess to the murder.

You shall offend him, and extend his passion.
Feed, and regard him not.—Are you a man?
MACBETH: Ay, and a bold one, that dare look on that
  Which might appal the devil.
LADY MACBETH: O proper stuff!   60
  This is the very painting of your fear.
  This is the air-drawn dagger which you said
  Led you to Duncan. O these flaws and starts,
  Impostors to true fear, would well become
  A woman's story at a winter's fire,
  Authorized by her grandam. Shame itself,
  Why do you make such faces? When all's done,
  You look but on a stool.
MACBETH: Prithee see there. Behold, look, lo, how say you?
  Why what care I? If thou canst nod, speak too.   70
  If charnel-houses and our graves must send
  Those that we bury back, our monuments
  Shall be the maws of kites.   [*Ghost disappears*
LADY MACBETH: What, quite unmanned in folly?
MACBETH: If I stand here, I saw him.
LADY MACBETH: Fie for shame!
MACBETH: Blood hath been shed ere now, i' th' olden time,
  Ere humane statute purged the gentle weal;
  Ay, and since too, murders have been performed
  Too terrible for the ear. The time has been,
  That when the brains were out, the man would die,
  And there an end. But now they rise again.   80
  With twenty mortal murders on their crowns,
  And push us from our stools. This is more strange
  Than such a murder is.
LADY MACBETH: My worthy lord,
  Your noble friends do lack you.
MACBETH: I do forget.
  Do not muse at me, my most worthy friends,

90–1   *And . . . here*. Is this a reckless challenge, a sincere wish, a deep fear
        i.e. rather Banquo than the thing that came?

91–2   *To . . . all*, i.e. good health to all.

93   *Avaunt*, hence, go away.
        According to stage tradition Macbeth here drops or throws
        down his goblet.

95   *speculation*, understanding, intelligence.

99   *What . . . dare*. Macbeth continues his former speech unheeding
        his wife's words beside himself with horror.

101   *armed*, i.e. with a horn. *Hyrcan*, Hyrcania, a former Persian
        province on the shores of the Black Sea.

102   *nerves*, sinews.

104   *dare . . . sword*, challenge me to a fight to the death, i.e. with no
        one to hinder us.

105   *If . . . then*. Several meanings have been suggested. If fear dwells in
        me then, or, if in fear I stay at home, seem to be the most likely.

106   *baby . . . girl*, (*a*) baby doll, (*b*) baby girl.

107–8   *Unreal . . . still*. Any gesture, change in pitch, speed and volume of
        voice, or change in breathing?

110   *admired disorder*, astonishing frenzy, i.e. disorder of the mind.

111   *overcome*, (*a*) pass over, (*b*) threaten.

112–

   13   *strange . . . owe*, feel a stranger to my own nature.

113   *owe*, possess.

I have a strange infirmity, which is nothing
To those that know me. Come, love and health to all,
Then I'll sit down. Give me some wine, fill full.
I drink to the general joy o' the whole table,
Enter GHOST

And to our dear friend Banquo, whom we miss;   90
Would he were here. To all, and him, we thirst,
And all to all.
LORDS: Our duties, and the pledge.
MACBETH: Avaunt, and quit my sight, let the earth hide thee!
Thy bones are marrowless, thy blood is cold;
Thou hast no speculation in those eyes
Which thou dost glare with!
LADY MACBETH: Think of this good peers,
But as a thing of custom. 'Tis no other,
Only it spoils the pleasure of the time.
MACBETH: What man dare, I dare.
Approach thou like the rugged Russian bear,   100
The armed rhinoceros, or the Hyrcan tiger;
Take any shape but that, and my firm nerves
Shall never tremble. Or be alive again,
And dare me to the desert with thy sword;
If trembling I inhabit then, protest me
The baby of a girl. Hence horrible shadow,
Unreal mockery, hence!   [*Ghost disappears*
                Why, so; being gone,
I am a man again. Pray you sit still.
LADY MACBETH: You have displaced the mirth, broke the
    good meeting
With most admired disorder.
MACBETH: Can such things be,   110
And overcome us like a summer's cloud,
Without our special wonder? You make me strange
Even to the disposition that I owe,

129

116   *mine*, i.e. natural ruby.

117–   *I . . . once*. Lady Macbeth fearing again that Macbeth will betray
20   himself quickly dismisses the guests.

119   *Stand . . . going*, do not stop for formal leave-taking. Knights
suggests that the break up of the feast symbolizes the social disorder of the kingdom.

     How do the guests depart—bewildered, suspicious, silent,
whispering, in groups, separately?

122   *It . . . blood*. A version of *Genesis*, ix. 6, 'Who so sheddeth man's
blood by man shall his blood be shed.'

     Ghosts in Elizabethan drama traditionally pleaded for revenge.

123   *Stones . . . move*, i.e. leaving the body of the murdered man un-
covered. *trees to speak*. Perhaps the story of the ghost of Polydorus
which spoke from a tree in the *Æneid*, iii. 22–68, prompted this,
though there are many stories of trees talking.

124   *Augures*, auguries, foretellings by the flight or feeding of birds.
understood relations, (*a*) hidden associations of things when rightly
interpreted, or (*b*) reports that could be understood because
delivered in human language (Schanzer).

125   *By . . . rooks*. Schanzer notes that all three birds can be taught to
speak, and thinks that Shakespeare was referring to the wide-
spread folk tale in which a bird denounces a crime. See *Pericles*,
IV. iii, 21–3. Shakespeare may have drawn on Lavater (See note
to l. 48) where a murderer wantonly destroyed a nest of swallows.
At supper his companions upbraided him and he replied; 'have
they not falsely accused me, a great while crying out on me that I
have murdered my father.' *magot-pies*, magpies. *choughs*, jackdaws,
rather than choughs.

126   *What . . . night?* A dull, flat question after a pause.

     Any movement or gesture?

127–9   *Almost . . . bidding?* Commentators see this as the turning point in
the construction of the play, Macbeth's relations with Macduff
balancing those with Banquo, and Macduff symbolically linked
with the coming of dawn.

128   *How say'st thou?* What do you say to this?

132   *fee'd*, in my pay. *I will tomorrow*. Muir suggests placing a colon
after tomorrow and interpreting, I will send to Macduff tomorrow.

135–6   *for . . . way*. Sisson's reading. This gives emphasis to the contradiction 'worst', 'good'.

136   *causes*, considerations.

When now I think you can behold such sights,
And keep the natural ruby of your cheeks,
When mine is blanched with fear.

ROSS: What sights, my lord?

LADY MACBETH: I pray you speak not; he grows worse and
    worse.

Question enrages him. At once, good night.
Stand not upon the order of your going.
But go at once.

LENNOX: Good night, and better health   120
Attend his Majesty.

LADY MACBETH: A kind good night to all.

                    [Exeunt all but Macbeth and Lady Macbeth

MACBETH: It will have blood, they say; blood will have blood.
Stones have been known to move, and trees to speak.
Augures and understood relations have
By magot-pies and choughs and rooks brought forth
The secret'st man of blood. What is the night?

LADY MACBETH: Almost at odds with morning, which is
    which.

MACBETH: How say'st thou, that Macduff denies his person
At our great bidding?

LADY MACBETH: Did you send to him sir?

MACBETH: I hear it by the way; but I will send.   130
There's not a one of them but in his house
I keep a servant fee'd. I will tomorrow,
And betimes I will, to the Weird Sisters.
More shall they speak; for now I am bent to know
By the worst means, the worst, for mine own good.
All causes shall give way. I am in blood

136–8　*I . . . o'er.* Macbeth is also at a turning point. Is he indifferent, callous, committed to evil, or contemptuous?

139　*Strange things,* e.g. the murder of Macduff.

140　*scanned,* come to light.

141　*season,* preserver. See II. ii, 35–43. Macbeth had murdered the healing sleep.

142　*self-abuse,* self-deception.

143　*initiate,* of a beginner.

144　*We . . . deed.* Does this line, isolated from the frame of Macbeth's couplets ll. 134–42, express—a statement of fact, hope of repentance, hellish resolve, or enjoyment of murder? How should it be spoken?

The heath

Most editors consider that this scene was not written by Shakespeare. Flatter, however, has argued strongly in favour of its authenticity. See Appendix III.

How should Hecate enter—by trap-door, normally by stage door, descend by stage-car, or appear on the balcony?

2　*beldams,* hags.

7　*close contriver,* secret creator.

11　*wayward son,* i.e. not committed to witchcraft.

15　*Acheron.* In classical myth a river in Hades, here, perhaps, Hell as implied by 'pit'.

Stepped in so far, that should I wade no more,
Returning were as tedious as go o'er.
Strange things I have in head, that will to hand;
Which must be acted ere they may be scanned.　　　140
LADY MACBETH: You lack the season of all natures, sleep.
MACBETH: Come, we'll to sleep. My strange and self-abuse
　　Is the initiate fear, that wants hard use.
　　We are yet but young in deed.　　　　　　　　[*Exeunt*

SCENE FIVE

Thunder. Enter the three WITCHES *meeting* HECATE

FIRST WITCH: Why how now Hecate, you look angerly.
HECATE: Have I not reason, beldams as you are,
　　Saucy and overbold? How did you dare
　　To trade and traffic with Macbeth
　　In riddles and affairs of death;
　　And I, the mistress of your charms,
　　The close contriver of all harms,
　　Was never called to bear my part,
　　Or show the glory of our art?
　　And, which is worse, all you have done　　　　10
　　Hath been but for a wayward son,
　　Spiteful, and wrathful, who, as others do,
　　Loves for his own ends, not for you.
　　But make amends now: get you gone,
　　And at the pit of Acheron
　　Meet me i' th' morning; thither he
　　Will come to know his destiny.

21   *dismal*, disastrous.

23–4 *Upon . . . profound*. In classical story a foam which was shed by the
      moon on certain earthly things when summoned by magic.
24   *profound*, (*a*) ready to fall, or (*b*) with hidden qualities.

27   *artificial sprites*, illusions, apparitions.

29   *confusion*, ruin, destruction.

31   *grace*, i.e. divine grace.
32   *security*, over-confidence.
S.D. *Come away*. A song 'Come away,' addressed to Hecate is found in
      Middleton's play *The Witch*, c. 1609.
34   *little spirit*, familiar spirit.
35   *foggy cloud*. A stage device of coloured cloths was sometimes used
      for clouds, here smoke may have been produced.
      What does this scene achieve—merely announces the next
      witches' sabbat, shows the mustering and declaration of the full
      force of evil against Macbeth who clings to his eternal jewel, makes
      the cauldron scene intelligible, prepares for Macbeth's psycho-
      logical development?

Another castle in Scotland

Should they meet or enter together?
   This scene is a kind of chorus: it sums up the situation, indicates the
change of mood in Macbeth's officers, and points out the gathering of the
forces of good.

3   *borne*, managed, handled.
4   *marry . . . dead*, i.e. Macbeth's pity came after Duncan's death.
      Variations in intonation are necessary to bring out the sarcasm
      and irony of Lennox's speech.

Your vessels and your spells provide,
Your charms, and every thing beside.
I am for the air; this night I'll spend   20
Unto a dismal and a fatal end.
Great business must be wrought ere noon:
Upon the corner of the moon
There hangs a vap'rous drop profound,
I'll catch it ere it come to ground;
And that distilled by magic sleights,
Shall raise such artificial sprites,
As by the strength of their illusion,
Shall draw him on to his confusion.
He shall spurn fate, scorn death, and bear   30
His hopes 'bove wisdom, grace, and fear;
And you all know security
Is mortals' chiefest enemy.
[*Music and a song within,* 'Come away, come away,' etc.
Hark! I am call'd; my little spirit, see,
Sits in a foggy cloud, and stays for me.   [*Exit*
FIRST WITCH: Come, let's make haste, she'll soon be back
    again.   [*Exeunt*

SCENE SIX

Enter LENNOX *and another* LORD

LENNOX: My former speeches have but hit your thoughts,
    Which can interpret further. Only I say
    Things have been strangely borne. The gracious Duncan
    Was pitied of Macbeth—marry he was dead.
    And the right-valiant Banquo walked too late,
    Whom you may say, if't please you, Fleance killed,

8   *who . . . thought*, who can fail to think. *monstrous*, unnatural.

10   *fact*, deed.

12   *pious*, righteous, loyal, i.e. to the divine Duncan. *delinquents*, i.e. those who fail in duty.
13   *thralls*, captives.
14   *Was . . . done?* Ironical.

17   *He . . . well*, (a) he has managed matters very well for himself, (b) his conduct has been very good.
19   *and 't*, if it.

20   *What 'twere*, what a crime it was.
21   *broad*, outspoken, plain.
22   *tyrant's*, (a) harsh king's, (b) usurper's.

25   *holds*, with-holds.

28–9   *That . . . respect*, that his misfortunes have in no way lessened the high respect that is paid him.

30   *upon his aid*, on his behalf.
31   *wake*, call to arms.

35   *Free . . . knives*, i.e. free our feasts and banquets from the threat of murder.
36   *faithful*, i.e. Macbeth was a usurper. *free*, i.e. that can be accepted with a free conscience.
38   *King*, Macbeth.

For Fleance fled—men must not walk too late.
Who cannot want the thought, how monstrous
It was for Malcolm and for Donalbain
To kill their gracious father? Damned fact.   10
How it did grieve Macbeth! Did he not straight
In pious rage the two delinquents tear,
That were the slaves of drink, and thralls of sleep?
Was not that nobly done? Ay, and wisely too;
For 'twould have angered any heart alive
To hear the men deny't. So that I say
He has borne all things well; and I do think
That had he Duncan's sons under his key—
As, and't please heaven, he shall not—they should find
What 'twere to kill a father. So should Fleance.   20
But peace—for from broad words, and 'cause he failed
His presence at the tyrant's feast, I hear
Macduff lives in disgrace. Sir, can you tell
Where he bestows himself?

LORD: The son of Duncan,
From whom this tyrant holds the due of birth,
Lives in the English Court, and is received
Of the most pious Edward with such grace,
That the malevolence of fortune nothing
Takes from his high respect. Thither Macduff
Is gone to pray the holy King, upon his aid   30
To wake Northumberland, and warlike Siward,
That by the help of these, with Him above
To ratify the work, we may again
Give to our tables meat, sleep to our nights,
Free from our feasts and banquets bloody knives,
Do faithful homage, and receive free honours,
All which we pine for now. And this report
Hath so exasperate the King, that he
Prepares for some attempt of war.

40   *with . . . I*, i.e. being met with an utter refusal from Macduff.

41   *cloudy*, sullen.

42   *hums*, mutters surlily. *rue*, regret, suffer for.

43   *clogs*, (*a*) delays, (*b*) burdens.

48   *suffering country*, i.e. country suffering.

Has the frequency of words suggesting holiness from l. 19—heaven, pious, pray, holy, Him above, holy angel, blessing, prayers—any significance?

What dramatic value have Lennox's sarcasm and pious wishes —to enlist the audience's sympathies with Malcolm's forces; to recapitulate with bitter condemnation Macbeth's deeds; to show the rise of antagonism among Macbeth's own followers; to place a valuation on the theme of false appearances?

LENNOX: Sent he to Macduff?
LORD: He did; and with an absolute 'Sir, not I',   40
  The cloudy messenger turns me his back,
  And hums, as who should say, 'You'll rue the time
  That clogs me with this answer.'
LENNOX: And that well might
  Advise him to a caution, to hold what distance
  His wisdom can provide. Some holy angel
  Fly to the Court of England, and unfold
  His message ere he come, that a swift blessing
  May soon return to this our suffering country
  Under a hand accursed.
LORD: I'll send my prayers with him.

                                          [*Exeunt*

The 'Pit of Acheron'

The entry of the witches and the cauldron through trap-doors on the main stage is accompanied by smoke and thunder. The actions and incantations of the Witches should be presented as a ritual.

1   *brinded*, brindled, streaked.

3   *Harpier*. A familiar spirit. Perhaps an owl, or simply a word derived from harpy.

8   *Sweltered venom*, sweated poison. The bitter, poisonous fluid found on the backs of toads.

10   *Double*. Perhaps suggesting deception as well as increase.

16   *fork*, forked tongue. *blind-worm's*, slow-worm's. The slow worm was formerly believed to be poisonous.

23   *mummy*, dried flesh. Flesh reputed to be from Egyptian mummies was in great demand as medicine. *maw and gulf*, stomach and gut.

24   *ravined*, (*a*) gorged, (*b*) ravenous, (*c*) ravening.

25   *digged i' th' dark*, i.e. to ensure that it had its full poisonous effect.

ACT FOUR

SCENE ONE

Thunder. Enter the three WITCHES

FIRST WITCH: Thrice the brinded cat hath mewed.
SECOND WITCH: Thrice and once the hedge-pig whined
THIRD WITCH: Harpier cries "Tis time, 'Tis time.'
FIRST WITCH: Round about the cauldron go;
  In the poisoned entrails throw.
  Toad, that under cold stone
  Days and nights hast thirty-one
  Sweltered venom sleeping got,
  Boil thou first i' th' charmed pot.
ALL: Double, double toil and trouble;   10
  Fire burn, and cauldron bubble.
SECOND WITCH: Fillet of a fenny snake,
  In the cauldron boil and bake;
  Eye of newt, and toe of frog,
  Wool of bat, and tongue of dog,
  Adder's fork, and blind-worm's sting,
  Lizard's leg, and howlet's wing,
  For a charm of powerful trouble,
  Like a hell-broth boil and bubble.
ALL: Double, double toil and trouble;   20
  Fire burn, and cauldron bubble.
THIRD WITCH: Scale of dragon, tooth of wolf,
  Witches' mummy, maw and gulf
  Of the ravined salt-sea shark,
  Root of hemlock digged i' th' dark,
  Liver of blaspheming Jew,

27   *yew*. Noted for its poisonous properties.

28   *slivered*, sliced or shaved off. *in . . . eclipse*. Things undertaken during an eclipse were thought to be threatened with disaster, unless they were evil schemes, which would prosper.

29   *Turk, Tartar's*. Both peoples were noted for their savage cruelty.

31   *drab*, prostitute.

32   *slab*, sticky, stodgy.

33   *chaudron*, entrails, guts.

34   *ingredience*. See I. vii, 11.
       The ingredients added by the Third Witch are linked with heathen evil, cruelty, poison, the unchristened, destroyed life, the broken parts of man and living creatures, i.e. disorder and chaos.

S.D.   *Hecate . . . Witches*. This entry notice and the five lines that follow are regarded as non-Shakespearian by most editors. Others suggest that 'and' in the entry notice should read 'to', or that the three additional witches were needed for the song. See Appendix III.

42   *elves and fairies*. Elves and fairies were usually associated with the black, white or grey spirits of sorcery and witchcraft. The fairies of *A Midsummer Night's Dream* were exceptional.

S.D.   *Black spirits, etc*. See Appendix III.

48   *black . . . hags*, i.e. who practise the Black Art (Muir).

50   *conjure*, call upon, summon. Macbeth himself acts as if he had the power of a necromancer. *by . . . profess*, i.e. sorcery, witchcraft. Should Macbeth reinforce his demands by gestures or postures?

53   *yesty*, frothing.

Gall of goat, and slips of yew
Slivered in the moon's eclipse,
Nose of Turk, and Tartar's lips,
Finger of birth-strangled babe   30
Ditch-delivered by a drab,
Make the gruel thick and slab.
Add thereto a tiger's chaudron,
For th' ingredience of our cauldron.
ALL: Double, double toil and trouble;
Fire burn, and cauldron bubble.
SECOND WITCH: Cool it with a baboon's blood,
Then the charm is firm and good.

Enter HECATE *and the three other* WITCHES

HECATE: O well done! I commend your pains,
And every one shall share i' th' gains.   40
And now about the cauldron sing,
Like elves and fairies in a ring,
Enchanting all that you put in.
                    [*Music and song*, 'Black spirits,' *etc.*
                    [*Exit Hecate*
SECOND WITCH: By the pricking of my thumbs,
Something wicked this way comes:
        Open, locks,
        Whoever knocks.

Enter MACBETH

MACBETH: How now, you secret, black, and midnight hags!
What is't you do?
ALL: A deed without a name.
MACBETH: I conjure you, by that which you profess,   50
Howe'er you come to know it, answer me.
Though you untie the winds and let them fight
Against the churches; though the yesty waves

143

54   *navigation*, shipping.

55   *bladed corn*, corn before the ear is formed. *lodged*, beaten flat.

57   *slope*, bend.

58–9 *treasure . . . together*, precious hidden seeds, from which come all created things, are thrown violently into disorder. See note to I. iii, 58.

60   *sicken*, grows tired of destroying.

       Macbeth recites as a kind of charm the powers of destruction by which he is summoning the witches to do his bidding. How should he pitch his voice?

65   *farrow*, litter, newly-born pigs.

S.D.   *armed head*. Various interpretations have been offered: (*a*) Macbeth's head, (*b*) Macduff, (*c*) Macdonwald, or perhaps the 'head of rebellion'.

69   *He . . . thought*. Ironical if the head is Macbeth's.

74   *harped*, put your finger on, touched on.

Confound and swallow navigation up;
Though bladed corn be lodged, and trees blown down;
Though castles topple on their warders' heads;
Though palaces and pyramids do slope
Their heads to their foundations; though the treasure
Of nature's germens tumble all together,
Even till destruction sicken; answer me   60
To what I ask you.

FIRST WITCH: Speak.

SECOND WITCH: Demand.

THIRD WITCH: We'll answer.

FIRST WITCH: Say if thou'dst rather hear it from our mouths,
Or from our masters?

MACBETH: Call 'em, let me see 'em.

FIRST WITCH: Pour in sow's blood, that hath eaten
Her nine farrow; grease that's sweaten
From the murderer's gibbet, throw
Into the flame.

ALL: Come high or low;
Thyself and office deftly show.

Thunder. FIRST APPARITION, *an armed head*

MACBETH: Tell me, thou unknown power—

FIRST WITCH: He knows thy thought.
Hear his speech, but say thou nought.   70

FIRST APPARITION: Macbeth, Macbeth, Macbeth, beware
Macduff;
Beware the Thane of Fife. Dismiss me. Enough.

                                            [*Descends*

MACBETH: Whate'er thou art, for thy good caution thanks;
Thou hast harped my fear aright. But one word more—

FIRST WITCH: He will not be commanded. Here's another,
More potent than the first.

S.D. *bloody child*, i.e. Macduff 'from his mother's womb untimely ripped'.

82 *Then . . . thee.* How should this be spoken—with relief, joy, doubt, or questioningly?

83–4 *I'll . . . fate.* He assumes that Macduff was 'born of woman', but he will make doubly certain by killing him and so compel fate to fulfil its promise.

84 *bond*, (*a*) agreement, (*b*) fetter.

85 *That . . . lies*, i.e. deny that there is any cause for fear.

86 *And . . . thunder*, i.e. profoundly. Perhaps a glance at witch-raised storms.

S.D. *child . . . hand*, (*a*) Malcolm, (*b*) James I.

All editors assume that Malcolm is intended in that he gives the order to hew down branches (V. iv, 4–5), but it could very well refer also to James I. It was well-known that James was crowned in the cradle, the tree could be a genealogical tree in keeping with the 'show' that follows. The word 'tree' unqualified was used in this sense, and pedigrees in this period were frequently depicted as trees.

87 *issue*, child.

88–9 *round And top*, the crown and very height.

93 *Great . . . hill.* Both are near Perth and some twelve miles apart.

95 *impress*, force to take up arms.

96 *bodements*, prophecies.

97–   *Rebellious . . . custom.* Editors suggest that these lines, particularly
  100 'our . . . Macbeth' are strange for Macbeth, but would be appropriate for one of the witches. However, Macbeth in his rapt and exulting pride may give his own view of the prophecy emphasized by rhyme.

97 *Rebellious dead.* This Folio reading fits Macbeth's thought, III. iv, 78–83, after the appearance of Banquo's ghost. See also V. ii, 3–5.

Theobald's emendation 'Rebellion's head' has many supporters. In this case Macbeth would have in mind the 'conspirers' of l. 91.

99 *live . . . nature*, live out his natural life. *pay*, yield.

100 *mortal custom*, natural death. Any movement or gesture?

Act Four, Scene One

Thunder. SECOND APPARITION, *a bloody child*

SECOND APPARITION: Macbeth, Macbeth, Macbeth!

MACBETH: Had I three ears, I'd hear thee.

SECOND APPARITION: Be bloody, bold and resolute; laugh
  to scorn

  The power of man, for none of woman born   80

  Shall harm Macbeth   [*Descends*

MACBETH: Then live Macduff, what need I fear of thee?

  But yet I'll make assurance double sure,

  And take a bond of fate. Thou shalt not live;

  That I may tell pale-hearted fear it lies,

  And sleep in spite of thunder.

Thunder. THIRD APPARITION, *a child crowned, with a tree in
his hand*

                   What is this,

  That rises like the issue of a king,

  And wears upon his baby brow the round

  And top of sovereignty?

ALL: Listen, but speak not to't.

THIRD APPARITION: Be lion-mettled, proud and take no
  care   90

  Who chafes, who frets, or where conspirers are.

  Macbeth shall never vanquished be, until

  Great Birnam wood to high Dunsinane hill

  Shall come against him.   [*Descends*

MACBETH: That will never be.

  Who can impress the forest, bid the tree

  Unfix his earth-bound root? Sweet bodements, good!

  Rebellious dead, rise never till the wood

  Of Birnam rise, and our high-placed Macbeth

  Shall live the lease of nature, pay his breath

  To time and mortal custom. Yet my heart   100

  Throbs to know one thing: tell me, if your art

106   *noise*, music, company of musicians.

110   *Show . . . heart*. An inverted proverb. Has this any significance?

111   *shadows*, appearances, images.

       Some gestures and movements by the witches to summon the show are required.

S.D.   *show . . . Kings*, i.e. the pedigree of James I, without his mother, Mary Queen of Scots. His pedigree was displayed on two pyramids in the Strand at the time of his first entry into London.

       Should these rise from a trap-door, enter normally on the stage, or move across the discovery space, or the balcony?

117   *crack*, trumpet blast, or thunder.

118   *I'll . . . more*. Any movement?

119   *glass*, a 'perspective' glass so cut as to produce illusions.

121   *twofold . . . sceptres*, i.e. two orbs, and the two sceptres used in the English coronation together with the one used in the Scottish coronation.

122–4 *Horrible . . . so?* Is Macbeth numb, shocked, frenzied, aghast, hysterical, despairing, or bitter?

123   *blood-boltered*, with hair clotted with blood.

125– *Ay . . . pay*. Regarded by editors as an addition by another
32   writer.

130   *antic round*, strange, outlandish round-dance.

131   *this great King*, (*a*) Macbeth, (*b*) King James.

Can tell so much, shall Banquo's issue ever
Reign in this kingdom?
ALL: Seek to know no more.
MACBETH: I will be satisfied. Deny me this,
　And an eternal curse fall on you. Let me know.
　Why sinks that cauldron, and what noise is this?   [*Oboes*
FIRST WITCH: Show!
SECOND WITCH: Show!
THIRD WITCH: Show!
ALL: Show his eyes, and grieve his heart;   110
　Come like shadows, so depart.

A show of eight KINGS, *the last with a glass in his hand*; BANQUO
following

MACBETH: Thou art too like the spirit of Banquo. Down!
　Thy crown does sear mine eyeballs; and thy hair,
　Thou other gold-bound brow, is like the first.
　A third is like the former. Filthy hags,
　Why do you show me this? A fourth? Start, eyes!
　What, will the line stretch out to th' crack of doom?
　Another yet? A seventh? I'll see no more.
　And yet the eighth appears, who bears a glass,
　Which shows me many more; and some I see   120
　That twofold balls and treble sceptres carry:
　Horrible sight! Now I see 'tis true,
　For the blood-boltered Banquo smiles upon me,
　And points at them for his. What, is this so?
FIRST WITCH: Ay sir, all this is so. But why
　Stands Macbeth thus amazedly?
　Come sisters, cheer we up his sprites,
　And show the best of our delights.
　I'll charm the air to give a sound,
　While you perform your antic round;   130
　That this great King may kindly say,

s.d. Is the dance slow, writhing, furious, or mocking? Do they vanish in smoke through trap-doors or through normal exits?

138 *Infected*, i.e. as with the plague.
139 *And . . . them*. Prophetic irony.
  A pause before Macbeth continues.

145 *flighty*, fleeting.

147–8 *firstlings . . . hand*, my heart's first plans shall be my hands' first actions.

152 *unfortunate*. Is Macbeth pitiful, savage, sadistic, or sardonic?
153 *trace*, follow, succeed.

155 *But . . . sights*, i.e. no more dealings with the witches—their evil work has been accomplished as his present intention shows.

Our duties did his welcome pay.

                  [Music. The Witches dance, and vanish

MACBETH: Where are they? Gone? Let this pernicious hour
  Stand aye accursed in the calendar.
  Come in, without there!

                 Enter LENNOX

LENNOX: What's your Grace's will?
MACBETH: Saw you the Weird Sisters?
LENNOX: No my lord.
MACBETH: Came they not by you?
LENNOX: No indeed my lord.
MACBETH: Infected be the air whereon they ride,
  And damned all those that trust them. I did hear
  The galloping of horse. Who was't came by?   140
LENNOX: 'Tis two or three, my lord, that bring you word
  Macduff is fled to England.
MACBETH: Fled to England?
LENNOX: Ay my good lord.
MACBETH: Time, thou anticipat'st my dread exploits.
  The flighty purpose never is o'ertook
  Unless the deed go with it. From this moment
  The very firstlings of my heart shall be
  The firstlings of my hand. And even now,
  To crown my thoughts with acts, be it thought and done.
  The castle of Macduff I will surprise,   150
  Seize upon Fife, give to the edge o' th' sword
  His wife, his babes, and all unfortunate souls
  That trace him in his line. No boasting like a fool;
  This deed I'll do before this purpose cool.
  But no more sights! Where are these gentlemen?
  Come bring me where they are.   *[Exeunt*

Macduff's castle

Lady Macduff's entry and movements should show her agitation. Is Ross pleading with her or gently rebuking her?

1   *What . . . land.* Identifies the speaker and shows her innocence of any plots.

3–4   *When . . . traitors,* i.e. Macduff has not done wrong, but the fear that made him fly to England is taken as evidence that he is a traitor. Does Lady Macduff believe he is a traitor—to Macbeth?

7   *titles,* possessions.

9   *wants . . . touch,* is without natural feelings of love.

12   *All . . . love.* See *I St. John,* iv. 18: 'There is no fear in love, but perfect love casteth out fear . . . he that feareth is not perfect in love'.
     Is Lady Macduff—scornful, indignant, bitter, tearful, impetuous, fearful, bewildered?.

15   *school,* control.

17   *fits,* crisis, danger points.

19   *know ourselves,* i.e. to be traitors.

19–22   *when . . . move,* our fears make us apt to believe in rumours; though we do not know what causes us to be afraid, our minds are tossed to and fro.

22   *Each . . . move.* The Folio reading. Many alterations have been suggested, e.g. 'none' for 'move', 'it moves' for 'and move', etc.

23   *Shall.* Ross is in a hurry.

25–6   *My . . . you.* Any gesture of farewell or blessing?

SCENE TWO

Enter LADY MACDUFF, *her* SON, *and* ROSS

LADY MACDUFF: What had he done, to make him fly the land?

ROSS: You must have patience madam.

LADY MACDUFF: He had none.
  His flight was madness. When our actions do not,
  Our fears do make us traitors.

ROSS: You know not
  Whether it was his wisdom, or his fear.

LADY MACDUFF: Wisdom! To leave his wife, to leave his
    babes,
  His mansion, and his titles in a place
  From whence himself does fly? He loves us not;
  He wants the natural touch. For the poor wren,
  The most diminutive of birds, will fight,   10
  Her young ones in her nest, against the owl.
  All is the fear, and nothing is the love;
  As little is the wisdom, where the flight
  So runs against all reason.

ROSS: My dearest coz,
  I pray you school yourself. But for your husband,
  He is noble, wise, judicious, and best knows
  The fits o' th' season. I dare not speak much further,
  But cruel are the times, when we are traitors,
  And do not know ourselves; when we hold rumour
  From what we fear, yet know not what we fear,   20
  But float upon a wild and violent sea
  Each way and move. I take my leave of you.
  Shall not be long but I'll be here again.
  Things at the worst will cease, or else climb upward
  To what they were before. My pretty cousin,
  Blessing upon you!

29   *my disgrace*, i.e. he would weep. *discomfort*, embarrassment.

30   *Sirrah . . . dead*. Is Lady Macduff standing, sitting, kneeling? Is her
      son on her knee, sitting on the floor or on a stool, or standing?
      your father's dead. Is she playful, serious, bitter, wry, teasing?

32-3 *As . . . they*. See *St. Matthew*, vi. 26 and xviii. 5–6.

32   *with . . . flies*. A grisly ironic prophecy?

34-5 *Poor . . . gin*, i.e. he would not survive long enough to fear the
      fowler's traps.

34   *lime*, bird-lime. A sticky substance smeared on twigs to entangle
      birds.

35   *gin*, trap, snare.

36   *Poor*, starved, thin. A quibble on 'poor' which should be stressed
      in speaking.

39-61 These lines with one or two exceptions are prose. Is this to give the
      effect of artless child's talk, or a sign of a topical reference added
      later?

41   *Then . . . again*, i.e. not 'for keeps' but merely to make a profit.

44   *Was . . . traitor*, i.e. as the earlier conversation, ll. 4, 18 might
      imply. Does Lady Macduff show any change of mood?

47-50 *one . . . hanged*. See II. iii, 7–10. Perhaps a glance at the trial and
      hanging of Garnet, or of Sir Everard Digby, a Gunpowder Plot
      conspirator, who wrote a pathetic poem to his son. If so, what
      dramatic value has it?

47   *one . . . lies*, i.e. an equivocator.

55-6 *Then . . . them*. Perhaps suggested by James' *Demonology*, p. 28,
      where the question is asked why, if witches have power over

LADY MACDUFF: Fathered he is, and yet he's fatherless.

ROSS: I am so much a fool, should I stay longer,
It would be my disgrace and your discomfort.
I take my leave at once.   [*Exit*

LADY MACDUFF: Sirrah, your father's dead,   30
And what will you do now? How will you live?

SON: As birds do mother.

LADY MACDUFF: What, with worms, and flies?

SON: With what I get I mean, and so do they.

LADYMACDUFF: Poor bird, thou'dst never fear the net nor lime,
The pitfall nor the gin.

SON: Why should I mother? Poor birds they are not set for.
My father is not dead, for all your saying.

LADY MACDUFF: Yes, he is dead. How wilt thou do for a
father?

SON: Nay, how will you do for a husband?

LADY MACDUFF: Why I can buy me twenty at any market. 40

SON: Then you'll buy 'em to sell again.

LADY MACDUFF: Thou speak'st with all thy wit, and yet i'
faith
With wit enough for thee.

SON: Was my father a traitor, mother?

LADY MACDUFF: Ay, that he was.

SON: What is a traitor?

LADY MACDUFF: Why one that swears, and lies.

SON: And be all traitors that do so?

LADY MACDUFF: Every one that does so is a traitor, and must
be hanged.   50

SON: And must they all be hanged that swear and lie?

LADY MACDUFF: Every one.

SON: Who must hang them?

LADY MACDUFF: Why, the honest men.

SON: Then the liars and swearers are fools; for there are liars and
swearers enow to beat the honest men, and hang up them.

death, they have not killed off all the good people. Bitter irony in view of what is imminent.

Is the boy pert, innocent, naive, clever, loyal, shrewd, wise beyond years?

What is the purpose of this conversation—to rouse pity, pathos, irony of condemning a good man, to convey her bitterness to her son who outwits her, to rouse tension as two doomed persons talk of their future?

Is the Messenger's entry hurried, stealthy, as if pursued?

63   *your . . . perfect*, I am perfectly aware of your high rank.
64   *doubt*, fear.

66   *little ones*. See note to ll. 32–3.
67   *To . . . savage*. How should Lady Macduff react?
68–9 *To . . . person*, to injure you would be a deed of fiercest cruelty, or 'to do worse' i.e. by not warning her.
      Why is the 'homely man' introduced—to intensify suspense, to show that goodness still exists?

72–4 *to . . . folly*. A bitter reversal of values.

76   *What . . . faces?* Possibly masks.

78   *unsanctified*. Macduff was in a sanctified place. See III. vi, 27–30.

80   *shag-eared*. Folio reading. Many editors prefer 'shag-haired' which occurs in 2 *Henry VI*, III. i, 367.

LADY MACDUFF: Now God help thee, poor monkey. But how
  wilt thou do for a father?
SON: If he were dead, you'd weep for him; if you would not, it
  were a good sign that I should quickly have a new father.   60
LADY MACDUFF: Poor prattler, how thou talk'st!

Enter a MESSENGER

MESSENGER: Bless you fair dame. I am not to you known,
  Though in your state of honour I am perfect.
  I doubt some danger does approach you nearly.
  If you will take a homely man's advice,
  Be not found here; hence with your little ones.
  To fright you thus, methinks I am too savage;
  To do worse to you were fell cruelty,
  Which is too nigh your person. Heaven preserve you,
  I dare abide no longer.   [*Exit*
LADY MACDUFF: Whither should I fly?   70
  I have done no harm. But I remember now
  I am in this earthly world, where to do harm
  Is often laudable, to do good sometime
  Accounted dangerous folly. Why then, alas,
  Do I put up that womanly defence,
  To say I have done no harm?

Enter MURDERERS

                        What are these faces?
FIRST MURDERER: Where is your husband?
LADY MACDUFF: I hope in no place so unsanctified
  Where such as thou mayst find him.
FIRST MURDERER: He's a traitor.
SON: Thou liest thou shag-eared villain.
FIRST MURDERER: What, you egg!   80
                                    [*Stabs him*

81   *fry*, young fish.
        How is the boy's body removed?
        Is the purpose of the whole scene to harrow the audience,
        blacken Macbeth by the bitterness of Lady Macduff's death, to
        show evil destruction at family level, to equate Macbeth with
        Herod in the slaughter of innocents?

England: the King's palace

Do the two men enter together or do they meet? Have they been talking
before?

3   *mortal*, deadly.

6–8   *Strike . . . dolour.* See ll. 223–5 and I. vii, 21–5.

8   *Like . . . dolour*, similar exclamation of grief. Some interjections
        were so classified.

10   *to friend*, to help me, on my side.

12   *sole*, very.
13   *honest*, honourable.
14–16   *something . . . lamb*, you may perceive something of his nature
        through his treatment of me, and therefore may see a kind of
        wisdom in sacrificing me (after Sisson). Editors generally prefer
        'deserve' for the Folio 'discerne'. i.e. that Macduff is seeking a
        reward from Macbeth for betraying Malcolm.
16   *To . . . lamb.* A grim reminder of the previous scene.
        Is Malcolm suspicious, cautious, sceptical, resentful, bitter,
        frank?
19   *recoil*, fall away, degenerate.
20   *imperial charge*, royal command.

Young fry of treachery !
SON: He has killed me mother,
Run away I pray you.   [*Dies*
               [*Exit Lady Macduff, crying* 'Murder !' *and*
                              pursued by the Murderers

SCENE THREE

Enter MALCOLM *and* MACDUFF

MALCOLM: Let us seek out some desolate shade, and there
Weep our sad bosoms empty.
MACDUFF: Let us rather
Hold fast the mortal sword, and like good men,
Bestride our down-fallen birthdom. Each new morn,
New widows howl, new orphans cry, new sorrows
Strike heaven on the face, that it resounds
As if it felt with Scotland, and yelled out
Like syllable of dolour.
MALCOLM: What I believe, I'll wail;
What know, believe; and what I can redress,
As I shall find the time to friend, I will.   10
What you have spoke, it may be so perchance.
This tyrant, whose sole name blisters our tongues,
Was once thought honest; you have loved him well;
He hath not touched you yet. I am young, but something
You may discern of him through me, and wisdom
To offer up a weak, poor, innocent lamb
T' appease an angry god.
MACDUFF: I am not treacherous.
MALCOLM: But Macbeth is.
A good and virtuous nature may recoil
In an imperial charge. But I shall crave your pardon.   20

21   *transpose*, change, alter.

22   *still*, always. *the brightest*, Lucifer, Satan.

23–4   *Though . . . so*, even though evil men to deceive others put on an appearance of virtue, yet good men must always keep their appearance of virtue unchanged. See I. v, 63–4, vii, 82.

24–5   *I . . . doubts*. Macduff hopes that Malcolm will lead an army against Macbeth; Malcolm suspects Maduff's integrity because he left his family in Scotland.

26   *rawness*, defencelessness, helplessness.

27   *motives*, causes of love.

28   *I pray you*. Any movement or reaction from Macduff?

29   *jealousies*, suspicions. *be your dishonours*, discredit you, i.e. my suspicions are to ensure my own safety not to discredit you.

33   *For . . . thee*. Is this a taunt? *wear . . . wrongs*, continue to flaunt your ill-gotten gains.

34   *title is affeered*, (*a*) your (tyranny's) possession of the crown is confirmed, (*b*) perhaps a quibble—the rightful title holder is afraid ('afeard').

37   *to boot*, as well.
       What movements are appropriate?

43   *gracious England*, Edward the Confessor.

45   *I . . . head*, i.e. as a serpent. Perhaps an echo of *Genesis*, iii. 15; *Romans*, xvi. 20. See Introduction, p. 22.

46   *wear . . . sword*, display it on my sword's point.

That which you are, my thoughts cannot transpose:
Angels are bright still, though the brightest fell.
Though all things foul would wear the brows of grace,
Yet grace must still look so.

MACDUFF: I have lost my hopes.

MALCOLM: Perchance even there where I did find my doubts.
    Why in that rawness left you wife and child,
    Those precious motives, those strong knots of love,
    Without leave-taking? I pray you,
    Let not my jealousies be your dishonours,
    But mine own safeties. You may be rightly just,   30
    Whatever I shall think.

MACDUFF: Bleed, bleed, poor country;
    Great tyranny, lay thou thy basis sure,
    For goodness dare not check thee; wear thou thy wrongs,
    The title is affeered. Fare thee well lord,
    I would not be the villain that thou think'st
    For the whole space that's in the tyrant's grasp,
    And the rich East to boot.

MALCOLM: Be not offended;
    I speak not as in absolute fear of you.
    I think our country sinks beneath the yoke;
    It weeps, it bleeds, and each new day a gash   40
    Is added to her wounds. I think withal,
    There would be hands uplifted in my right;
    And here from gracious England have I offer
    Of goodly thousands. But, for all this,
    When I shall tread upon the tyrant's head,
    Or wear it on my sword, yet my poor country
    Shall have more vices than it had before,
    More suffer, and more sundry ways than ever,
    By him that shall succeed.

MACDUFF: What should he be?

MALCOLM: It is myself I mean; in whom I know   50

51 *grafted*, implanted, imbedded.
52 *opened*, i.e. as buds.

55 *confineless harms*, boundless vices.

58 *Luxurious*, lustful.
59 *Sudden*, violent.

63 *cistern*, pit, pool, in Shakespeare usually containing toads and snakes.
64 *continent*, (*a*) restraining, (*b*) chaste.
65 *will*, desire, lust.
66–7 *Boundless . . . tyranny*, natural desires when uncontrolled tyrannize the kingdom of man's being. See note I. 1, s.d.

71 *Convey*, secretly arrange.
72 *cold*, chaste. *time*, present state of affairs, world.

75 *dedicate*, offer.

77 *ill-composed affection*, unbalanced nature.
78 *staunchless*, ever greedy, unquenchable.
79 *cut off*, kill.
80 *his*, this man's.

All the particulars of vice so grafted,
That when they shall be opened, black Macbeth
Will seem as pure as snow, and the poor state
Esteem him as a lamb, being compared
With my confineless harms.

MACDUFF: Not in the legions
Of horrid hell can come a devil more damned
In evils, to top Macbeth.

MALCOLM: I grant him bloody,
Luxurious, avaricious, false, deceitful,
Sudden, malicious, smacking of every sin
That has a name. But there's no bottom, none,   60
In my voluptuousness. Your wives, your daughters,
Your matrons, and your maids, could not fill up
The cistern of my lust, and my desire
All continent impediments would o'erbear,
That did oppose my will. Better Macbeth
Than such a one to reign.

MACDUFF: Boundless intemperance
In nature is a tyranny; it hath been
Th' untimely emptying of the happy throne,
And fall of many kings. But fear not yet
To take upon you what is yours: you may   70
Convey your pleasures in a spacious plenty,
And yet seem cold, the time you may so hoodwink.
We have willing dames enough; there cannot be
That vulture in you, to devour so many
As will to greatness dedicate themselves,
Finding it so inclined.

MALCOLM: With this, there grows
In my most ill-composed affection, such
A staunchless avarice, that were I King,
I should cut off the nobles for their lands,
Desire his jewels and this other's house,   80

85   *pernicious root*. Perhaps a glance at the love of money is the root of all evil, 1 *Timothy*, vi. 10.

86   *summer-seeming*, summer-like, i.e. (*a*) short-lived, (*b*) hot.

87   *sword*, death.

88   *foisons*, abundance.

89   *mere own*, own possessions. *portable*, bearable.

90   *With . . . weighed*, i.e. when they are balanced against your graces.

95   *relish*, taste, trace.

96   *division*, variation, separate parts. *several*, separate.

98–   *Pour . . . earth*. Paul thinks this is a topical reference to the noisy
100 mob during Concordia's address to James and Christian of Denmark at Cheapside, 31 July, 1606. It may rather owe something to the *Litany*: '. . . give to all nations unity, peace, and concord' or the 'Prayer for the Church Militant': . . . 'inspire continually the universal Church with the spirit of truth, unity and concord'.

98   *milk of concord*. See I. v, 15.

99   *confound*, destroy.

100   *O Scotland, Scotland*. Does Macduff turn away, hide his face, or raise his arms?

104   *untitled*, usurping.

107   *By . . . accursed*, is accursed by his own declared debarring from the throne.

       Most editors read 'accursed' for the Folio, 'accust'. Muir prefers 'accus'd'.

108   *blaspheme his breed*, speak evil that dishonours the sanctity of his parentage. The phrase is emphatic. Contrast 'truest issue', l. 106.

       Personal sins of avarice and lechery can be overlooked, but Malcolm's rejection of the qualities a king should use in his divine office of ruling the people, and his threat to destroy the divine, peaceful order of the whole universe are so diabolically evil that they blast Macduff's hopes.

108– *Thy . . . lived*. Shakespeare departs from Holinshed in sanctifying
11   Malcolm's parents.

And my more-having would be as a sauce
To make me hunger more, that I should forge
Quarrels unjust against the good and loyal,
Destroying them for wealth.
MACDUFF: This avarice
  Sticks deeper, grows with more pernicious root
  Than summer-seeming lust; and it hath been
  The sword of our slain kings; yet do not fear;
  Scotland hath foisons to fill up your will,
  Of your mere own. All these are portable,
  With other graces weighed.   90
MALCOLM: But I have none. The king-becoming graces,
  As justice, verity, temp'rance, stableness,
  Bounty, perseverance, mercy, lowliness,
  Devotion, patience, courage, fortitude,
  I have no relish of them, but abound
  In the division of each several crime,
  Acting it many ways. Nay, had I power, I should
  Pour the sweet milk of concord into hell,
  Uproar the universal peace, confound
  All unity on earth.
MACDUFF: O Scotland, Scotland!   100
MALCOLM: If such a one be fit to govern, speak.
  I am as I have spoken.
MACDUFF: Fit to govern?
  No, not to live. O nation miserable,
  With an untitled tyrant bloody-sceptered,
  When shalt thou see thy wholesome days again,
  Since that the truest issue of thy throne
  By his own interdiction stands accursed,
  And does blaspheme his breed? Thy royal father
  Was a most sainted King; the Queen that bore thee,
  Oftener upon her knees than on her feet,   110

111   *Died . . . lived*, i.e. was dead to worldly things and spent each day in prayer. See 1 *Corinthians*, xv. 31 'I die daily'.

112–   *These . . . Scotland*. It is these very evils in Macbeth, which you
     13   now confess are also your own which have driven me from Scotland.

113–   *O . . . passion*. What gestures and movements by both would be
     14   appropriate?

116   *scruples*, doubts.

118   *trains*, devices, plots.

120–1   *God . . . me*. This may be an echo of Jonathan's visit to David who had fled from court to warn him of Saul's murderous designs: 'the Lord be between me and thee' 1 *Samuel*, xx. 23, 42. There are other similarities of situation in the same chapter.

123   *Unspeak . . . detraction*, withdraw what I have said against myself, i.e. the qualities that do not become a king are used to establish Malcolm's standing.

125   *For*, as.

134   *Siward*, Earl of Northumberland, of Danish parentage.

135   *at a point*, in readiness, fully prepared.

136–7   *the . . . quarrel*, may the chance that goodness will prevail be in accordance with the justice of our cause.

137–9   *Why . . . reconcile*. Is Macduff suspicious, angry at being deceived, deeply emotional?

Died every day she lived. Fare thee well,
These evils thou repeat'st upon thyself
Hath banished me from Scotland. O my breast,
Thy hope ends here.

MALCOLM: Macduff, this noble passion,
  Child of integrity, hath from my soul
  Wiped the black scruples, reconciled my thoughts
  To thy good truth and honour. Devilish Macbeth
  By many of these trains hath sought to win me
  Into his power; and modest wisdom plucks me
  From over-credulous haste; but God above   120
  Deal between thee and me. For even now
  I put myself to thy direction, and
  Unspeak mine own detraction; here abjure
  The taints and blames I laid upon myself,
  For strangers to my nature. I am yet
  Unknown to woman, never was forsworn,
  Scarcely have coveted what was mine own,
  At no time broke my faith, would not betray
  The devil to his fellow, and delight
  No less in truth than life. My first false speaking   130
  Was this upon myself. What I am truly,
  Is thine, and my poor country's, to command;
  Whither indeed, before thy here-approach,
  Old Siward, with ten thousand warlike men
  Already at a point, was setting forth.
  Now we'll together, and the chance of goodness
  Be like our warranted quarrel. Why are you silent?

MACDUFF: Such welcome and unwelcome things at once
  'Tis hard to reconcile.

Enter a DOCTOR

MALCOLM: Well, more anon. Comes the King forth, I pray
  you?   140

142   *stay*, await.
142-3 *convinces . . . art*, defeats the utmost attempts of the medical art.
143   *great . . . art*. Contrast III. v, 9, the 'glory of our art' that leads to destruction.
145   *presently*, immediately.

146   *evil*, scrofula, the king's evil.

149   *solicits*, moves by prayers. Contrast Macbeth's 'supernatural soliciting' I. iii, 130.
150   *strangely-visited*, afflicted with unnatural diseases.

153   *golden stamp*, gold coin, an 'angel'.

156   *virtue*, power.
157   *heavenly . . . prophecy*. Contrast that of the witches.

159   *grace*, divine grace.
       The gifts of curing the king's evil by touch and of prophesying were recorded of the saintly Edward the Confessor. King James made much of his touch for the evil in that it proved his royal descent.
       What is the point of this account—to balance the evil magic of the witches, to show the healing gifts of the holy king, to hint at and contrast with the incurable sickness of Scotland, V. iii, 50–6, or is it to compliment James 1?
160   *My countryman*, i.e. recognizable by his dress. *but . . . not*, (a) I cannot see who it is, (b) I do not know whether he is friend or foe.

167   *once*, at any time.

DOCTOR: Ay sir, there are a crew of wretched souls
   That stay his cure. Their malady convinces
   The great assay of art; but at his touch,
   Such sanctity hath heaven given his hand,
   They presently amend.
MALCOLM: I thank you doctor.   [*Exit Doctor*
MACDUFF: What's the disease he means?
MALCOLM: 'Tis called the evil:
   A most miraculous work in this good King,
   Which often since my here-remain in England
   I have seen him do. How he solicits heaven,
   Himself best knows; but strangely-visited people,   150
   All swollen and ulcerous, pitiful to the eye,
   The mere despair of surgery, he cures,
   Hanging a golden stamp about their necks.
   Put on with holy prayers; and 'tis spoken,
   To the succeeding royalty he leaves
   The healing benediction. With this strange virtue,
   He hath a heavenly gift of prophecy,
   And sundry blessings hang about his throne,
   That speak him full of grace.

Enter ROSS

MACDUFF: See who comes here.   160
MALCOLM: My countryman; but yet I know him not.
MACDUFF: My ever-gentle cousin, welcome hither.
MALCOLM: I know him now. Good God, betimes remove
   The means that makes us strangers.
ROSS: Sir, amen.
MACDUFF: Stands Scotland where it did?
ROSS: Alas poor country,
   Almost afraid to know itself. It cannot
   Be called our mother, but our grave; where nothing
   But who knows nothing is once seen to smile;

168   *rent*, rend.

170   *modern ecstasy*, everyday feeling, sham frenzy.
        Paul notes that James was concerned to expose fraudulent demoniacs who threw themselves into sham trances.

173   *Dying . . . sicken*, i.e. killed before they have time to be ill.

174   *Too nice*, too detailed.

175   *hiss the speaker*, i.e. for telling out-of-date and inaccurate news.
176   *teems*, gives birth to.

177   *well*. Frequently used of dead persons. See *Antony and Cleopatra*, II. v, 32–3.
179   *well at peace*. Is Ross's quibbling—to avoid telling Macduff before he is prepared, to ease his own emotions, to provide suspense in the audience?
180   *Be . . . speech*. Macduff is irritated at Ross's sudden, brief replies.
181–2 *tidings . . . borne*, i.e. the murder of Macduff's wife and children.
183   *out*, in arms against Macbeth.

185   *power*, forces.

188   *doff*, throw off.

192   *gives out*, proclaims, tells of.
194   *would*, ought to.

Where sighs, and groans, and shrieks that rent the air,
Are made, not marked; where violent sorrow seems
A modern ecstasy. The dead man's knell   170
Is there scarce asked for who, and good men's lives
Expire before the flowers in their caps,
Dying or ere they sicken.
MACDUFF: O relation
  Too nice, and yet too true!
MALCOLM: What's the newest grief?
ROSS: That of an hour's age doth hiss the speaker.
  Each minute teems a new one.
MACDUFF: How does my wife?
ROSS: Why well.
MACDUFF: And all my children?
ROSS: Well too.   177
MACDUFF: The tyrant has not battered at their peace?
ROSS: No, they were well at peace, when I did leave 'em.
MACDUFF: Be not a niggard of your speech. How goes't?
ROSS: When I came hither to transport the tidings,
  Which I have heavily borne, there ran a rumour
  Of many worthy fellows that were out;
  Which was to my belief witnessed the rather,
  For that I saw the tyrant's power a-foot.
  Now is the time of help; your eye in Scotland
  Would create soldiers, make our women fight,
  To doff their dire distresses.
MALCOLM: Be't their comfort
  We are coming thither. Gracious England hath
  Lent us good Siward, and ten thousand men;   190
  An older and a better soldier none
  That Christendom gives out.
ROSS: Would I could answer
  This comfort with the like. But I have words
  That would be howled out in the desert air,

195   *latch*, catch.

196   *The general cause*, everybody in general. *fee-grief*, sorrow peculiar to one person.

202   *possess*, inform.

203   *Hum*. A sigh or groan.

206   *quarry*, the heap of dead bodies. *deer*, (*a*) deer, (*b*) dear ones.

207   *To . . . you*, i.e. the shock would be the death of you too.

208   *What . . . brows*. What actions of Macduff have led up to this?

209–   *grief . . . break*. A proverbial saying probably borrowed with
10   rhymes from Florio's translation of a line from Seneca's *Hippolytus*. What value has the rhyme?

210   *o'er fraught*, over-burdened.
       How should the repeated questions be said—softly, harshly, slowly, with incredulity, agonizingly?

214–   *medicines . . . grief*, i.e. the healing that Malcolm is to bring to
15   Scotland.

216   *He . . . children*. Does this refer to Malcolm, for making a suggestion no father would make; to Macbeth who has no children on whom revenge can be taken; or to Macbeth, who if he had children, would not have committed this crime?

218   *dam*, (*a*) mother, (*b*) dame.

219   *fell*, fierce, deadly. *swoop*, continuance of the 'kite' image.

Where hearing should not latch them.

MACDUFF: What concern they?
   The general cause? Or is it a fee-grief
   Due to some single breast?

ROSS: No mind that's honest
   But in it shares some woe; though the main part
   Pertains to you alone.

MACDUFF: If it be mine,
   Keep it not from me, quickly let me have it.   200

ROSS: Let not your ears despise my tongue for ever,
   Which shall possess them with the heaviest sound
   That ever yet they heard.

MACDUFF: Hum! I guess at it.

ROSS: Your castle is surprised; your wife and babes
   Savagely slaughtered. To relate the manner,
   Were on the quarry of these murdered deer
   To add the death of you.

MALCOLM: Merciful heaven!
   What man, ne'er pull your hat upon your brows,
   Give sorrow words; the grief that does not speak
   Whispers the o'er-fraught heart, and bids it break.   210

MACDUFF: My children too?

ROSS: Wife, children, servants, all
   That could be found.

MACDUFF: And I must be from thence!
   My wife killed too?

ROSS: I have said.

MALCOLM: Be comforted.
   Let's make us medicines of our great revenge,
   To cure this deadly grief.

MACDUFF: He has no children. All my pretty ones?
   Did you say all? O hell-kite! All?
   What, all my pretty chickens and their dam
   At one fell swoop?

220   *Dispute*, fight against, stand up to.

223–7   *Did . . . now*. Macduff's speech here, in ll. 230–5 and in II. iii, 61–3 is deeply religious in tone. His painful, doubting question is resolved by a humble admission that his sins have brought punishment on his family. Macduff turns from the others as in a soliloquy.

225   *Naught*, wicked.

226   *demerits*, faults.

227   *Heaven . . . now*. Any gesture from Macduff and the others?

232   *intermission*, delay.

236   *power*, army.

237   *Our . . . leave*, all we need is to take our leave.

238–9   *powers . . . instruments*, (*a*) arm themselv es, (*b*) set on their followers, i.e. himself, etc. Contrast II. i, 7.

239   *cheer*, encouragement.

     Is the purpose of this scene—to show the 'foul is fair' motive in reverse, to establish Malcolm's fitness for kingship, to describe the ideal king and the loyal subject (Macduff), to encourage the audience's condemnation of Macbeth's crimes seen in a national light, to act as a chorus commentary?

MALCOLM: Dispute it like a man.

MACDUFF: I shall do so;   220
But I must also feel it as a man:
I cannot but remember such things were
That were most precious to me. Did heaven look on,
And would not take their part? Sinful Macduff,
They were all struck for thee. Naught that I am,
Not for their own demerits, but for mine,
Fell slaughter on their souls. Heaven rest them now.

MALCOLM: Be this the whetstone of your sword, let grief
Convert to anger; blunt not the heart, enrage it.   229

MACDUFF: O I could play the woman with mine eyes,
And braggart with my tongue. But gentle heavens,
Cut short all intermission. Front to front
Bring thou this fiend of Scotland and myself;
Within my sword's length set him, if he scape,
Heaven forgive him too.

MALCOLM: This tune goes manly.
Come go we to the King; our power is ready,
Our lack is nothing but our leave. Macbeth
Is ripe for shaking, and the powers above
Put on their instruments. Receive what cheer you may,
The night is long that never finds the day.   240

                                        [*Exeunt*

Macbeth's castle

Who enters first? Is the Doctor angry, fretful, sceptical? Is the Gentle-woman insistent, anxious, pleading, urgent?

3 *into the field*, i.e. against rebels. See IV. iii, 183.

4 *nightgown*, dressing-gown.

5 *closet*, a case or chest for personal valuables. *fold it*. Probably to mark a margin (Muir). *write upon't*. Perhaps a confession.

8 *perturbation in nature*, upset in her health, disturbance of her con-stitution.

9 *the . . . watching*, the things she would do when awake.

10 *slumbery agitation*, activity while asleep. The phrase emphasizes the paradox in the previous sentence.

12–15 *That . . . speech*. Is this the Gentlewoman's caution, a device to raise suspense, or to prepare the audience for speech from a sleep-walker?

16 *guise*, way she appears.

18 *close*, hidden. Where should they hide—by a pillar supporting the canopy, in the discovery space or by an entrance? Is Lady Macbeth on the stage, balcony or in the discovery space?

   Is her walk dragging, laboured, slow, quick, hesitant, like a blind person?

20–1 *she . . . command*, i.e. through fear of the dark or is it a symbol of her groping for spiritual light.

20–3 *She . . . shut*. See *St. Luke*, xi. 34–6.

23 *sense*. Plural.

24–5 *What . . . hands*. What has she done with the taper?

ACT FIVE

SCENE ONE

Enter a DOCTOR OF PHYSIC *and a* WAITING GENTLEWOMAN

DOCTOR: I have two nights watched with you, but can perceive
no truth in your report. When was it she last walked?

GENTLEWOMAN: Since his Majesty went into the field, I have
seen her rise from her bed, throw her nightgown upon her,
unlock her closet, take forth paper, fold it, write upon't, read
it, afterwards seal it, and again return to bed; yet all this while
in a most fast sleep.   7

DOCTOR: A great perturbation in nature, to receive at once
the benefit of sleep, and do the effects of watching. In this
slumbery agitation, besides her walking, and other actual performances, what at any time have you heard her say?

GENTLEWOMAN: That sir, which I will not report after her.

DOCTOR: You may to me, and 'tis most meet you should.

GENTLEWOMAN: Neither to you nor any one, having no wit-
ness to confirm my speech.   15

Enter LADY MACBETH *with a taper*

Lo you, here she comes. This is her very guise, and upon my
life fast asleep.

Observe her, stand close.

DOCTOR: How came she by that light?

GENTLEWOMAN: Why it stood by her. She has light by her
continually, 'tis her command.   21

DOCTOR: You see her eyes are open.

GENTLEWOMAN: Ay but their sense are shut.

DOCTOR: What is it she does now? Look how she rubs her
hands.

29 *Yet . . . spot.* See II. ii, 46–7, 60–1, 67.

30 *set down,* i.e. on his 'tables' or notebook using pen and inkhorn.

31 *satisfy,* support.

32 *damned spot,* i.e. (*a*) blood that the 'little water' cleared, (*b*) the Devil's mark.

32–3 *One . . . do't.* Is this a clock or the bell? See II. i, 31–2.

33 *Hell is murky.* Is this horror or acceptance?

35–6 *Yet . . . him.* An unexpected horror.

38 *The . . . wife.* Is this hysterical, sardonic, babyish sing song, plain statement?

40 *starting,* i.e. the flaws and starts of III. iv, 63.

41 *You, you,* Lady Macbeth.

44 *smell.* Another unexpected horror.

45 *Arabia.* Formerly the source of spices and scents.

45–6 *Oh, oh, oh !* Sighs or groans, not exclamations of surprise.

47 *sorely charged,* heavily burdened.

49 *dignity,* worth.

56–7 *I . . . grave.* Macbeth's terrible dreams apparently continued after Banquo's death.

GENTLEWOMAN: It is an accustomed action with her, to seem thus washing her hands. I have known her continue in this a quarter of an hour.

LADY MACBETH: Yet here's a spot.

DOCTOR: Hark! she speaks. I will set down what comes from her, to satisfy my remembrance the more strongly.   31

LADY MACBETH: Out damned spot, out I say! One, two; why then 'tis time to do't. Hell is murky. Fie my lord, fie! A soldier, and afeard? What need we fear who knows it, when none can call our power to account? Yet who would have thought the old man to have had so much blood in him?

DOCTOR: Do you mark that?

LADY MACBETH: The Thane of Fife had a wife; where is she now? What, will these hands ne'er be clean? No more o' that my lord, no more o' that: you mar all with this starting.   40

DOCTOR: Go to, go to! You have known what you should not.

GENTLEWOMAN: She has spoke what she should not, I am sure of that. Heaven knows what she has known.

LADY MACBETH: Here's the smell of the blood still; all the perfumes of Arabia will not sweeten this little hand. Oh, oh, oh!

DOCTOR: What a sigh is there! The heart is sorely charged.

GENTLEWOMAN: I would not have such a heart in my bosom for the dignity of the whole body.

DOCTOR: Well, well, well.   50

GENTLEWOMAN: Pray God it be sir.

DOCTOR: This disease is beyond my practice. Yet I have known those which have walked in their sleep who have died holily in their beds.

LADY MACBETH: Wash your hands, put on your nightgown, look not so pale. I tell you yet again Banquo's buried; he cannot come out on's grave.

DOCTOR: Even so?

LADY MACBETH: To bed, to bed; there's knocking at the gate.

60–61   *What's . . . undone.* See III. ii, 12.

64   *Foul . . . abroad,* rumours of evil deeds are spreading.
65   *infected,* i.e. with evil.
67   *divine,* priest.
69   *annoyance,* means of injuring herself. A pointer to Lady Macbeth's suicide.
71–2   *My . . . speak.* Spoken to himself as he goes off.
71   *mated,* bewildered.

       Why does the Doctor now use verse?

       Is the value of this scene—to blacken Macbeth to the audience by recapitulating his crimes, to dispose of Lady Macbeth as the lesser criminal, to symbolize the corruption of Scotland (see V. iii, 39–56), or to symbolize Macbeth's own mind? Does Lady Macbeth reveal fear, horror, guilt, remorse, madness, delirium?

Near Dunsinane

The ominous burst of drumming, noise of marching and entry of battle flags is a sharp contrast with the previous scene.

2   *uncle Siward.* Paul notes that Shakespeare corrects Holinshed who describes Siward as Malcolm's grandfather.
3   *Revenges,* the desire for revenge. *dear,* deeply felt.
4   *to . . . alarm,* i.e. to warfare.
5   *Excite . . . man,* rouse the dead. *mortified man,* (a) dead man, (b) man who has renounced his natural feelings, a hermit.

Come, come, come, come, give me your hand. What's done
cannot be undone. To bed, to bed, to bed.   61

[Exit

DOCTOR: Will she go now to bed?

GENTLEWOMAN: Directly.

DOCTOR: Foul whisperings are abroad. Unnatural deeds
   Do breed unnatural troubles; infected minds
   To their deaf pillows will discharge their secrets.
   More needs she the divine than the physician.
   God, God forgive us all. Look after her,
   Remove from her the means of all annoyance,
   And still keep eyes upon her. So, good night: 70
   My mind she has mated, and amazed my sight.
   I think, but dare not speak.

GENTLEWOMAN: Good night good doctor.

[Exeunt

SCENE TWO

Enter, with drum and colours, MENTEITH, CAITHNESS, ANGUS,
LENNOX, *and* SOLDIERS

MENTEITH: The English power is near, led on by Malcolm,
   His uncle Siward, and the good Macduff.
   Revenges burn in them; for their dear causes
   Would to the bleeding and the grim alarm
   Excite the mortified man.

ANGUS: Near Birnam wood
   Shall we well meet them; that way are they coming.

CAITHNESS: Who knows if Donalbain be with his brother?

LENNOX: For certain sir, he is not. I have a file
   Of all the gentry; there is Siward's son,

10   *unrough*, beardless.

11   *Protest . . . manhood*, show forth their manhood for the first time.

13–14 *Some . . . fury*. Perhaps a hint that 'whom the gods would destroy
      they first make mad'.

15   *distempered cause*, sick cause, i.e. like a diseased body.

15–16 *He . . . rule*, (*a*) he cannot control his evil passions, (*b*) he cannot
      restrain his subjects from rebelling against his sick cause.

16–17 *Now . . . hands*, A vivid reminder. See II. ii, 60–1; V. i, 39, 44–5.

18   *minutely*, every moment. *upbraid*, denounce. *faith-breach*, treason.

19   *in command*, because they are ordered to do so.

21–2 *Hang . . . thief*. Clothing images occur elsewhere in the play, I. iii,
      108–9, 145. For a similar shrinking see 1 *Henry IV*, V. iv, 87, 'ill-
      weaved ambition how much art thou shrunk'.

23   *pestered*, troubled. *recoil*, give away. *start*. An echo of III. iv, 63;
      V. i, 40.

24–5 *When . . . there*, i.e. like his kingdom his own nature revolts
      against him.

27   *the . . . weal*, i.e. Malcolm.

28–9 *pour . . . us*, we will shed every drop of our blood to purge our
      country of its sickness. (*a*) shed their blood in battle, (*b*) be bled to
      cure an illness. The healing and purging image occurs elsewhere
      in the play.

30   *To . . . flower*, to make grow the flower of kings, Malcolm. *dew*.
      Perhaps an antidote to Hecate's vaporous drop profound. *sovereign*,
      (*a*) royal, (*b*) healing.

31   *Birnam*. Ominous and emphatic.

And many unrough youths, that even now   10
  Protest their first of manhood.
MENTEITH: What does the tyrant?
CAITHNESS: Great Dunsinane he strongly fortifies.
  Some say he's mad; others, that lesser hate him,
  Do call it valiant fury; but for certain,
  He cannot buckle his distempered cause
  Within the belt of rule.
ANGUS: Now does he feel
  His secret murders sticking on his hands.
  Now minutely revolts upbraid his faith-breach;
  Those he commands move only in command,
  Nothing in love. Now does he feel his title   20
  Hang loose about him, like a giant's robe
  Upon a dwarfish thief.
MENTEITH: Who then shall blame
  His pestered senses to recoil, and start,
  When all that is within him does condemn
  Itself for being there?
CAITHNESS: Well, march we on,
  To give obedience where 'tis truly owed.
  Meet we the medicine of the sickly weal,
  And with him pour we, in our country's purge,
  Each drop of us.
LENNOX: Or so much as it needs,
  To dew the sovereign flower, and drown the weeds.   30
  Make we our march towards Birnam.   [*Exeunt marching*

Macbeth's castle

S.D.   Does Macbeth enter—furiously, despondently, frantically, fearfully? Does his speech show him as reckless, contemptuous, raging, indifferent, boastful?

1   *them*, i.e. his thanes.

2   *Birnam . . . Dunsinane*. This now raises suspense after Lennox's last words, and shows Macbeth's state of mind.

3   *taint*, dishonour myself, rot.

4   *spirits*, i.e. the apparitions.

5   *consequences*, actions and their results, relations of things.

8   *English epicures*. A phrase of contempt. *epicures*, those who pursue pleasure particularly in eating. A popular misunderstanding of the teaching of the Greek philosopher, Epicurus.

9   *sway*, rule myself.

11   *The . . . black*, i.e. devils were supposed to be black. *loon*, rogue, clot. Babcock suggests that 'loon', grebe or diver, is glanced at here earlier than the N.E.D. records. He points out the linkage of ideas, cream-faced—loon (white below black above)—goose—lily-livered—patch (on cloth)—linen—whey-face.

15   *lily-livered*. The liver was supposed to be the seat of courage. A pale, bloodless liver was a sign of a coward. *patch*, (*a*) fool, (*b*) patch on cloth, (*c*) plaster.

17   *counsellors to fear*, put fear into the minds of others. *whey*, liquid left after milk curdles.

19   *Take . . . hence*. Does Macbeth manhandle, kick, threaten or push away—the servant?

19–   *I . . . not*. Is this spoken in confidence to the audience, or to
   28 himself? Where is the Doctor?

20   *When I behold*, i.e. fear in his followers. *push*, crisis, effort, attack.

21   *cheer*, (*a*) hearten, (*b*) enthrone (a quibble on 'chair').

23   *sear*, withered. Muir quotes Onions, 'withered state'.

SCENE THREE

Enter MACBETH, DOCTOR, *and* ATTENDANTS

MACBETH: Bring me no more reports, let them fly all.
Till Birnam wood remove to Dunsinane,
I cannot taint with fear. What's the boy Malcolm?
Was he not born of woman? The spirits that know
All mortal consequences have pronounced me thus:
'Fear not Macbeth, no man that's born of woman
Shall e'er have power upon thee.' Then fly false thanes,
And mingle with the English epicures.
The mind I sway by, and the heart I bear,
Shall never sag with doubt, nor shake with fear.   10

Enter a SERVANT
The devil damn thee black, thou cream-faced loon.
Where gott'st thou that goose look?
SERVANT: There is ten thousand—
MACBETH: Geese, villain?
SERVANT: Soldiers sir.
MACBETH: Go prick thy face, and over-red thy fear,
Thou lily-livered boy. What soldiers, patch?
Death of thy soul, those linen cheeks of thine
Are counsellors to fear. What soldiers, whey-face?
SERVANT: The English force, so please you.
MACBETH: Take thy face hence.   [*Exit Servant*
                          Seyton!—I am sick at heart,
When I behold—Seyton, I say!—This push   20
Will cheer me ever, or disseat me now.
I have lived long enough. My way of life
Is fallen into the sear, the yellow leaf;
And that which should accompany old age,
As honour, love, obedience, troops of friends,

27   *mouth-honour,* lip service. *breath,* i.e. mere air.

28   *fain,* gladly.

       Does this speech reveal—self-pity, regret, dignity, despair, maudlin sentiment, recognition of hell?

34   *I'll . . . on.* Is this impatience, irresolution, fear, loss of control?

35   *moe,* more. *horses,* i.e. horsemen. *skirr,* scour.

37   *How . . . doctor?* Macbeth has ignored the doctor so far. Is he indifferent to his wife's illness?

39   *Cure . . . that.* Perhaps a negative gesture from the Doctor.

40–5   *Canst . . . heart.* Kocher quotes Bright, *Treatise of Melancholy,* that for a guilty consience 'no medicine, no purgation, no cordiall, no tryacle or balme are able to assure the afflicted soul and trembling heart, now panting under the terrors of God'.

40   *minister to,* (*a*) treat medically, (*b*) give spiritual help to.

42   *written . . . brain,* i.e. the troubles imprinted on the mind.

43   *oblivious,* bringing forgetfulness.

44   *perilous stuff,* care, sorrow, melancholy.

45–6   *Therein . . . himself,* i.e. it is not melancholy or madness but the working of conscience (Kocher).

47   *Throw . . . it.* James I constantly gibed at doctors.

50–1   *cast The water,* diagnose disease by examining urine.

52   *purge . . . health.* See for contrast V. ii, 27–8.

I must not look to have; but in their stead
Curses, not loud but deep, mouth-honour, breath,
Which the poor heart would fain deny, and dare not.
Seyton!

Enter SEYTON

SEYTON: What's your gracious pleasure?
MACBETH: What news more?
SEYTON: All is confirmed my lord, which was reported.   31
MACBETH: I'll fight, till from my bones my flesh be hacked.
   Give me my armour.
SEYTON: 'Tis not needed yet.
MACBETH: I'll put it on.
   Send out moe horses, skirr the country round,
   Hang those that talk of fear. Give me mine armour.
   How does your patient, doctor?
DOCTOR: Not so sick my lord,
   As she is troubled with thick-coming fancies
   That keep her from her rest.
MACBETH: Cure her of that.
   Canst thou not minister to a mind diseased,   40
   Pluck from the memory a rooted sorrow,
   Raze out the written troubles of the brain,
   And with some sweet oblivious antidote
   Cleanse the stuffed bosom of that perilous stuff
   Which weighs upon the heart?
DOCTOR: Therein the patient
   Must minister to himself.
MACBETH: Throw physic to the dogs, I'll none of it.
   Come, put mine armour on; give me my staff.
   Seyton, send out. Doctor, the thanes fly from me.
   Come sir, dispatch. If thou couldst, doctor, cast   50
   The water of my land, find her disease,
   And purge it to a sound and pristine health,

54   *Pull't . . . say*. In his agitation he is putting on and taking off his armour and throwing orders to Seyton.

55   *cyme*, tender tops of colewort, or of any plant. Many editors prefer 'senna', the reading of the Fourth Folio.

58   *Bring . . . me*, i.e. helmet or sword.

59–60 *I . . . Dunsinane*. A jingle to fortify himself.

61–2 *Were . . . here*. The Doctor's rhyme with its realistic self-interest caps Macbeth's.

Birnam wood

Again heavy drumming and quickening marching and display of battle flags. The entry should perhaps be made from the right-hand entry now associated with Malcolm's forces. Macbeth and his soldiers can enter from the left-hand entry—associated with hell-mouth in the older plays. Any stage properties required?

2   *chambers . . . safe*. A reference to Duncan's murder. i.e. when a man can go to bed and sleep in safety.

6   *discovery*, scouting, reconnaissance.

9   *endure*, hold out against, stand.

10   *Our . . . 't*, a siege by us.

I would applaud thee to the very echo,
That should applaud again. Pull't off I say.
What rhubarb, cyme, or what purgative drug,
Would scour these English hence? Hear'st thou of them?
DOCTOR: Ay my good lord; your royal preparation
   Makes us hear something.
MACBETH: Bring it after me.
   I will not be afraid of death and bane,
   Till Birnam forest come to Dunsinane.   60
                              [*Exeunt all but Doctor*
DOCTOR: Were I from Dunsinane away, and clear,
   Profit again should hardly draw me here.   [*Exit*

SCENE FOUR

Enter, with drum and colours, MALCOLM, SIWARD *and* YOUNG
   SIWARD, MACDUFF, MENTEITH, CAITHNESS, ANGUS,
      LENNOX, ROSS, *and* SOLDIERS, *marching*

MALCOLM: Cousins, I hope the days are near at hand
   That chambers will be safe.
MENTEITH: We doubt it nothing.
SIWARD: What wood is this before us?
MENTEITH: The wood of Birnam.
MALCOLM: Let every soldier hew him down a bough,
   And bear't before him, thereby shall we shadow
   The numbers of our host, and make discovery
   Err in report of us.
SOLDIERS: It shall be done.
SIWARD: We learn no other but the confident tyrant
   Keeps still in Dunsinane, and will endure
   Our setting down before't.
MALCOLM: 'Tis his main hope.   10

189

11 *advantage*, favourable opportunity. *gone*, Johnson's suggestion for the Folio 'given' which may have been 'caught' by the compositor from the next line.

12 *more and less*, nobles and common people.

14–15 *Let . . . event*, to see whether our views are accurate let us wait until the battle makes them clear.

18 *What . . . owe*, i.e. our gains and losses.

19 *Thoughts . . . relate*, guesses may express false hopes.

20 *certain . . . arbitrate*, a definite result can only be decided by battle.

Dunsinane

S.D. The drum beats may be different in pitch and style from those of Malcolm's army.

1 *Hang . . . walls*, i.e. on the balcony.

4 *ague*, fever.

5 *forced*, (*a*) reinforced, (*b*) stuffed (i.e. as roast game is stuffed). This continues contemptuously the image of eating.

7 *home*, thoroughly.

9 *I . . . fears*. The desolate eeriness of the cry reminded him of former fears.

10 *cooled*, frozen, become numb.

11 *fell of hair*, scalp.

12 *dismal treatise*, horrifying story.

13 *supped . . . horrors*. Is this from 'our poisoned chalice' (I. vii, 11), or from the banquet (III. iv).

14 *Direness*, horror.

15 *start*, frighten. See note to V. ii, 23.

For where there is advantage to be gone,
Both more and less have given him the revolt,
And none serve with him but constrained things,
Whose hearts are absent too.

MACDUFF: Let our just censures
Attend the true event, and put we on
Industrious soldiership.

SIWARD: The time approaches
That will with due decision make us know
What we shall say we have, and what we owe.
Thoughts speculative their unsure hopes relate,
But certain issue strokes must arbitrate;   20
Towards which advance the war.   [*Exeunt, marching*

SCENE FIVE

Enter, with drum and colours, MACBETH, SEYTON, *and* SOLDIERS

MACBETH: Hang out our banners on the outward walls.
The cry is still 'They come'. Our castle's strength
Will laugh a siege to scorn. Here let them lie
Till famine and the ague eat them up.
Were they not forced with those that should be ours,
We might have met them dareful, beard to beard,
And beat them backward home.   [*A cry of women within*
                        What is that noise?

SEYTON: It is the cry of women, my good lord.   [*Exit*

MACBETH: I have almost forgot the taste of fears.
The time has been, my senses would have cooled   10
To hear a night-shriek, and my fell of hair
Would at a dismal treatise rouse and stir
As life were in't. I have supped full with horrors;
Direness, familiar to my slaughterous thoughts
Cannot once start me.

17–18   *She . . . word.* Is Macbeth callous, indifferent, insensitive, regretful, abrupt, heartbroken? Accordingly how should these words be spoken?

17   *hereafter*, later, sometime, at a fitter time.

18   *a . . . word*, a proper time to die. See *Ecclesiastes*, iii. 2.

19   *Tomorrow . . . tomorrow*, i.e. a meaningless succession of days in the hereafter.

20   *petty*, trivial, insignificant.

21   *recorded time*, (*a*) book of time, (*b*) i.e. until judgement day.

22–3   *all . . . death*. From the meaninglessness of the future he turns to the inanity of the past.

22   *lighted*, i.e. by daylight.

23   *candle*. See Introduction, p. 23. Is this a link with Lady Macbeth's 'light'?

24   *Life's . . . shadow*. For the image compare *Ecclesiastes*, vi. 12; viii. 13, and particularly *Job*, viii. 9, 'For we are but of yesterday, and consider not that our days upon earth are but a shadow'. *poor player*, (*a*) bad actor, (*b*) pitiful actor.

    See *A Midsummer Night's Dream*, V. i, 209, 'The best in this kind are but shadows'.

25   *struts and frets*. Contemptuous. Compare *Measure for Measure*, II. ii, 118.

26–7   *It . . . Told*. See *Psalms*, xc. 9, 'We bring our years to an end as it were a tale that is told'.

28   *Signifying nothing*. Is Macbeth 'fey', an atheist, equivocating, deluded, logical, Satan's mouthpiece?

    The soliloquy is the consummation of all Macbeth represents. Its images are closely linked, e.g. hereafter—Tomorrow—day—recorded time—yesterdays; lighted—candle—shadow—player; and there are other associations. There are, too, numerous echoes of the Bible. What effect does this have—solemnity, gravity, dignity, verity, persuasiveness, self-deception, desperation?

29   *Thou . . . tongue*. The Messenger finds difficulty in speaking apart from breathlessness.

35   *Liar and slave*. Any action?

40   *cling*, shrivel.

42   *I . . . resolution*, I draw back in courage. *pull in*, rein back, withdraw.

    Macbeth turns to the audience. What has he done with the Messenger?

Act Five, Scene Five

Enter SEYTON
Wherefore was that cry?

SEYTON: The Queen, my lord, is dead.

MACBETH: She should have died hereafter;
There would have been a time for such a word.
Tomorrow, and tomorrow, and tomorrow,
Creeps in this petty pace from day to day,   20
To the last syllable of recorded time;
And all our yesterdays have lighted fools
The way to dusty death. Out, out, brief candle!
Life's but a walking shadow, a poor player,
That struts and frets his hour upon the stage,
And then is heard no more. It is a tale
Told by an idiot, full of sound and fury,
Signifying nothing.

Enter a MESSENGER
Thou comest to use thy tongue. Thy story quickly.

MESSENGER: Gracious my lord,   30
I should report that which I say I saw,
But know not how to do't.

MACBETH: Well, say sir.

MESSENGER: As I did stand my watch upon the hill,
I looked toward Birnam, and anon methought
The wood began to move.

MACBETH: Liar and slave!

MESSENGER: Let me endure your wrath, if't be not so.
Within this three mile may you see it coming.
I say, a moving grove.

MACBETH: If thou speak'st false,
Upon the next tree shalt thou hang alive
Till famine cling thee. If thy speech be sooth,   40
I care not if thou dost for me as much.
I pull in resolution, and begin

42–5   *begin . . . Dunsinane.* Spoken emphatically with growing emphasis.

46   *out,* i.e. Macbeth leaves the security of his castle.

47   *avouches,* swears is true.

49   *aweary . . . sun,* i.e. (*a*) the daily round, (*b*) kingship.

50   *estate . . . undone,* the whole universe were disrupted. See III. ii, 16.

51   *Blow . . . wrack.* Macbeth is not repentant. Macbeth invokes storms, the signs of disorder in the universe.

52   *harness,* armour.

Before the castle

The roll of drums is almost continuous and increasing in intensity.

2   *uncle,* Siward.

4   *first battle,* main army.

10   *harbingers,* heralds.

To doubt th' equivocation of the fiend,
That lies like truth: 'Fear not, till Birnam wood
Do come to Dunsinane'; and now a wood
Comes toward Dunsinane. Arm, arm, and out!
If this which he avouches does appear,
There is nor flying hence, nor tarrying here.
I 'gin to be aweary of the sun,
And wish th' estate o' th' world were now undone.   50
Ring the alarum bell! Blow wind, come wrack,
At least we'll die with harness on our back.   *[Exeunt*

SCENE SIX

Enter, with drum and colours, MALCOLM, SIWARD, MACDUFF,
etc., and their Army, with boughs

MALCOLM: Now near enough; your leafy screens throw down,
And show like those you are. You, worthy uncle,
Shall with my cousin your right noble son,
Lead our first battle. Worthy Macduff and we
Shall take upon's what else remains to do,
According to our order.
SIWARD: Fare you well.
Do we but find the tyrant's power tonight,
Let us be beaten, if we cannot fight.
MACDUFF: Make all our trumpets speak, give them all breath,
Those clamorous harbingers of blood and death. *[Exeunt.*
                                        Alarums

Before the castle

The noises of battle and the rushing to and fro of soldiers accompany the drumming.

Is Macbeth drooping, wounded, savage, snarling, despondent, beast-like?

1   *They . . . stake*, i.e. like a bear to be baited by dogs.

2   *course*, bout, round. *What's he*, what kind of a person is he.

5   *What . . . name*. A fierce shout after a swift entry.

7, 8   *hell, devil*. A repeated association of Macbeth with hell.

10–11   *with . . . lie*, i.e. as it were a trial by combat.

s.d.   The fight should be a skilful demonstration of sword-play.

11   *Thou . . . woman*. How spoken: triumphantly, regretfully, sneeringly, or confidently?

s.d.   *Enter Macduff*. The timing of this entry increases suspense. Macduff is now hard on Macbeth's heels.

17   *kerns*, i.e. mercenaries.

18   *staves*, spears. *Either thou, Macbeth*, either I fight you Macbeth.

20   *undeeded*, unused.

SCENE SEVEN

Alarums. Enter MACBETH

MACBETH: They have tied me to a stake; I cannot fly,
But bear-like I must fight the course. What's he
That was not born of woman? Such a one
Am I to fear, or none.

Enter YOUNG SIWARD

YOUNG SIWARD: What is thy name?

MACBETH: Thou'lt be afraid to hear it.

YOUNG SIWARD: No; though thou call'st thyself a hotter name
Than any is in hell.

MACBETH: My name's Macbeth.

YOUNG SIWARD: The devil himself could not pronounce a title
More hateful to mine ear.

MACBETH: No, nor more fearful.

YOUNG SIWARD: Thou liest, abhorred tyrant, with   my
sword   10
I'll prove the lie thou speak'st.

                          [*They fight, and young Siward is slain*

MACBETH: Thou wast born of woman.
But swords I smile at, weapons laugh to scorn,
Brandished by man that's of a woman born.   [*Exit*

Alarums. Enter MACDUFF

MACDUFF: That way the noise is. Tyrant, show thy face.
If thou be'st slain, and with no stroke of mine,
My wife and children's ghosts will haunt me still.
I cannot strike at wretched kerns, whose arms
Are hired to bear their staves. Either thou, Macbeth,
Or else my sword, with an unbattered edge
I sheath again undeeded. There thou shouldst be;   20

20–2 *There . . . bruited*, i.e. appropriate noises off.
22   *bruited*, announced.
s.d.   Malcolm's entry should be formal with ceremony. Macbeth's banners should be hauled down.

24   *gently rendered*, easily captured, readily surrendered.

27   *The . . . yours*, you have almost won the day.
       Siward stresses the ease with which the castle has been captured. Should he stand beside his son's body or has it been removed?

29   *strike beside us*, (*a*) fight with us, or, (*b*) purposely miss us with their blows.

The battleground before the castle

Is Macbeth battered, exhausted, dejected, brisk, alert?

1–2   *Why . . . sword*, i.e. by suicide like Brutus or Antony.
2–3   *whiles . . . them*. Any movement?
2   *lives*, living men.
3   *hell-hound*. See V. vii, 6, 7.

5–6   *my . . . already*. Is this remorse, fear, or guilt?
5   *charged*, (*a*) burdened, (*b*) accused.

7   *My . . . sword*, my sword is my answer.

8   *terms*, words.
s.d.   *They fight*. Again some impressive sword-play.

9   *intrenchant*, that cannot be cut, invulnerable.

By this great clatter, one of greatest note
Seems bruited. Let me find him, fortune,
And more I beg not.   [*Exit. Alarums*

Enter MALCOLM *and* SIWARD

SIWARD: This way my lord, the castle's gently rendered.
  The tyrant's people on both sides do fight;
  The noble thanes do bravely in the war;
  The day almost itself professes yours,
  And little is to do.
MALCOLM: We have met with foes
  That strike beside us.
SIWARD: Enter sir, the castle.
                    [*Exeunt. Alarum*

SCENE EIGHT

Enter MACBETH

MACBETH: Why should I play the Roman fool, and die
  On mine own sword? Whiles I see lives, the gashes
  Do better upon them.

Enter MACDUFF

MACDUFF: Turn hell-hound, turn!
MACBETH: Of all men else I have avoided thee.
  But get thee back, my soul is too much charged
  With blood of thine already.
MACDUFF: I have no words:
  My voice is in my sword, thou bloodier villain
  Than terms can give thee out!   [*They fight*
MACBETH: Thou losest labour;
  As easy mayst thou the intrenchant air
  With thy keen sword impress, as make me bleed.   10

12   *must not*, is fated not to.

13   *Despair thy charm*, lose all trust in your charm.

14   *angel*, i.e. evil angel. *still*, ever.

16   *Untimely ripped*, i.e. by Cæsarean section, cutting through the body wall. This short line may indicate a pause before Macbeth speaks.
        Any change in Macbeth's tones and demeanour?

18   *better . . . man*, spirit, manhood.

19   *juggling*, deceitful.

20   *palter*, deal crookedly, equivocate.

23   *coward*, Is he?

24–7   *And . . . tyrant*. Is Macbeth being offered his life?

24   *show . . . time*, spectacle of the age.

26   *Painted . . . pole*, painted on a board or cloth which hung from a pole as advertisement.

32   *try the last*, (*a*) test the last prophecy, (*b*) fight to a finish.

33, 34 *Macduff, enough*. Perhaps an ominous echo of the first apparition's warning, IV. i, 71–2.

S.D.   The Folio directions have caused debate. They may be intended to suggest a long, arduous fight. Wilson suggests that Macbeth is killed in the discovery space and concealed by the curtain. Most editors doubt the directions, and have Macbeth killed 'off'. Do you agree? See Introduction, p. 33.

Let fall thy blade on vulnerable crests;
I bear a charmed life, which must not yield
To one of woman born.
MACDUFF: Despair thy charm,
And let the angel whom thou still hast served
Tell thee, Macduff was from his mother's womb
Untimely ripped.
MACBETH: Accursed be that tongue that tells me so,
For it hath cowed my better part of man.
And be these juggling fiends no more believed,
That palter with us in a double sense;   20
That keep the word of promise to our ear,
And break it to our hope. I'll not fight with thee.
MACDUFF: Then yield thee coward,
And live to be the show and gaze o' th' time.
We'll have thee, as our rarer monsters are,
Painted upon a pole, and underwrit,
'Here may you see the tyrant.'
MACBETH: I will not yield
To kiss the ground before young Malcolm's feet,
And to be baited with the rabble's curse.
Though Birnam wood be come to Dunsinane,   30
And thou opposed, being of no woman born,
Yet I will try the last. Before my body
I throw my warlike shield. Lay on Macduff,
And damned to him that first cries 'Hold, enough!'
                              [*Exeunt, fighting. Alarums*
              Enter fighting and MACBETH *slain*

Courtyard of the castle

S.D. The trumpets are heard signalling the end of the battle, followed by a fanfare to herald the full ceremonial entrance of Malcolm.
How is Malcolm placed—above the others, centre stage back, or well forward?

2–3 *Some . . . bought.* Sadly ironical.
2 *go off*, be killed. *by these*, i.e. numbers of men who are safe.

8 *unshrinking station*, the post he defended without flinching.

14 *hairs.* A pun on 'heirs' has been suggested.

18 *parted*, died. *paid his score*, did his duty (paid his debts).
This story was well-known. Paul suggests that its insertion here was as a compliment to the Danish king (Siward was of Danish blood).

20–1 *Behold . . . head*, i.e. on a pole, or on his sword. See IV. iii, 46.

SCENE NINE

Retreat. Flourish. Enter, with drum and colours, MALCOLM, SIWARD,
ROSS, LENNOX, ANGUS, CAITHNESS, MENTEITH,
and SOLDIERS

MALCOLM: I would the friends we miss were safe arrived.
SIWARD: Some must go off; and yet by these I see,
  So great a day as this is cheaply bought.
MALCOLM: Macduff is missing, and your noble son.
ROSS: Your son my lord, has paid a soldier's debt:
  He only lived but till he was a man,
  The which no sooner had his prowess confirmed
  In the unshrinking station where he fought,
  But like a man he died.
SIWARD: Then he is dead?
ROSS: Ay, and brought off the field. Your cause of sorrow
  Must not be measured by his worth, for then   11
  It hath no end.
SIWARD: Had he his hurts before?
ROSS: Ay, on the front.
SIWARD: Why then, God's soldier be he.
  Had I as many sons as I have hairs,
  I would not wish them to a fairer death.
  And so, his knell is knolled.
MALCOLM: He's worth more sorrow,
  And that I'll spend for him.
SIWARD: He's worth no more.
  They say he parted well, and paid his score.
  And so God be with him. Here comes newer comfort.

Re-enter MACDUFF, *with* MACBETH'S *head*
MACDUFF: Hail King, for so thou art. Behold where stands   20

21   *The . . . free*, the age has recovered its freedom.

22   *compassed . . . pearl*, surrounded by the flower of your kingdom's nobility (like pearls on a crown).

25   *Hail . . . Scotland*. Any gestures?

27–8 *reckon . . . you*, reward you for your loyalty, and so pay our debts to you.

31   *planted . . . time*, established at the beginning of this new era.

34   *Producing forth*, seeking out.

35   *butcher . . . queen*. Do you agree?

38   *grace of Grace*. See *St. John*, i. 16 and Introduction, p. 23.

39   *in measure*, suitably, appropriately.
      A full ceremonial exit.

Th' usurper's cursed head. The time is free.
I see thee compassed with thy kingdom's pearl,
That speak my salutation in their minds;
Whose voices I desire aloud with mine:
Hail King of Scotland!

ALL: Hail King of Scotland!   [*Flourish*

MALCOLM: We shall not spend a large expense of time,
Before we reckon with your several loves,
And make us even with you. My thanes and kinsmen,
Henceforth be earls, the first that ever Scotland
In such an honour named. What's more to do,   30
Which would be planted newly with the time—
As calling home our exiled friends abroad,
That fled the snares of watchful tyranny,
Producing forth the cruel ministers
Of this dead butcher, and his fiend-like queen,
Who as 'tis thought, by self and violent hands
Took off her life—this, and what needful else
That calls upon us, by the grace of Grace,
We will perform in measure, time and place.
So thanks to all at once, and to each one,   40
Whom we invite to see us crowned at Scone.

                              [*Flourish. Exeunt*

APPENDICES

I

THE SOURCES OF *MACBETH*

MANY works have been put forward as possible sources of themes and passages in *Macbeth*. Gwenn's *Tres Sybillae* produced at Oxford 1605 in which three prophetesses hailed James, was itself suggested by the greeting of the 'weird sisters' in *Holinshed*, and may have directed Shakespeare's attention to the story of Macbeth.

Daniel's *Queen's Arcadia*, 1605, and Seneca's *Agamemnon* and *Hercules Furens* provided passages which Shakespeare imitated consciously or not.

Erasmus' *Colloquia* may have prompted the comparison between men and dogs (III. i, 92–100); De Loier's *Treatise of Spectres* (tr. 1605) may have led to the introduction of Banquo's ghost at the feast; and even the bloody hands theme, it is alleged, may owe something to Deloney's *Thomas of Reading*, 1600, or to the *Faerie Queene*. Some of these appear unnecessary and improbable, and in any case are of little help in considering the impact of the play. The frequent echoes of the *Bible*, particularly from *Revelation*, carry with them a different significance, and are discussed in the Introduction, pp. 20–3.

Attempts have also been made to show that Shakespeare was influenced by the works of James I. *The Counterblast to Tobacco*, *Basilikon Doron*, *True Law of Free Monarchies*, *A Fruitful Meditation*, *Demonology* have been cited as providing information and ideas that Shakespeare embodied in the play. While he probably did draw on the *Demonology* for details of witchcraft, his use of the other works is less certain and of a more general kind. As the play was obviously intended as a compliment to James, it is to be expected that Shakespeare made himself familiar with the considered opinions of the royal patron of his company.

A marked feature of the play is the parallels between it and Shakespeare's earlier works: the *Rape of Lucrece*, *2 Henry VI*, and *Richard III*. These may rise from the similarity of themes. Certainly from *Titus Andronicus* and the *Rape of Lucrece* to *Pericles* lust and murder appear as blood-brothers (II. i, 52–6 and Introduction, p. 16). Again, the parallels between *Macbeth* and 2 *Henry VI* are, as Muir suggests, 'probably due to the fact that the theme of witchcraft called up the earlier associations'. The resemblances between *Richard III* and *Macbeth* may spring from deliberate parallelism. As Shakespeare had shown the triumph of the House of Tudor over the evil, usurping Richard, so he showed the triumph of an ancestor of the Scottish royal house over the evil, usurping Macbeth.

The historical source of *Macbeth* is Holinshed's *Chronicle*, 1587, though there is reason to suppose that Shakespeare was acquainted with Buchanan's *Rerum Scoticarum Historia*, 1582, and Leslie's *De Origine, Moribus, et Rebus Gestis Scotorum*, Buchanan may have suggested Macbeth's motives for murdering Banquo, the jeering at Macbeth by his wife, and Macbeth's reception of the creation of Malcolm Prince of Cumberland. Leslie may have given the material for the show of eight kings—though Shakespeare could have obtained this elsewhere—and he refers to Duncan as the most holy king. These are not strong claims, and such motivation may well have developed naturally from Holinshed's account. Together with the other works mentioned before, they do indicate that Shakespeare was sensitive to current opinions, was well-read and had a retentive memory, and took care to read extensively the material bearing on a story he proposed to dramatize.

Shakespeare's very free alterations and additions to the story in Holinshed are most helpful as pointers to his dramatic methods and intentions. It is fair to say that Holinshed provides the barest outline of the story. The dialogue between Macduff and Malcolm in IV. iii is the closest the play stands to the words of the *Chronicle*. Shakespeare's additions are considerable.

Lady Macbeth and all her invocations, her arguments, her somnambulism and suicide are derived from Holinshed's single reference to her that she 'lay sore upon him (Macbeth) to attempt this thing, as she that was very ambitious, burning in unquenchable desire to bear the name of a Queen', and from the earlier account of the murder of Duff by Donwald whose wife showed him the means whereby he might do the deed.

Macbeth in the *Chronicle* meets the three Weird Sisters whose prophecies are like those in the play except that they declare that Macbeth shall come to an unlucky end and have no heir, and that Banquo's descendants shall rule Scotland. This happens before the rebellion and invasion. Later he 'learned of certain wizards, in whose words he put great confidence' (because of the truth of the earlier prophecy of the sisters) that Macduff was a danger to him, but a 'certain witch' told him that he could not be slain by man born of woman nor defeated until Birnam Wood came to Dunsinane, otherwise he would have slain Macduff. To this Shakespeare added the incantations of the witches, the cauldron scene, Hecate, the apparitions, and the show of eight kings.

Some scenes owe nothing at all to the *Chronicle*: the banquet with the appearance of Banquo's ghost; the conversation between Lady Macduff and her son, Ross, the Messenger and the Murderers; the Porter's scene; Macbeth's conversation with the Murderers and with Banquo (III. i); and the conversation between Lennox and a Lord (III. vi) except for the news of Macduff's flight to England.

Shakespeare also made a number of alterations and omissions: The three campaigns against Macdonwald, Sweno and Canute are compressed into one. Paul notes that mention of Sweno's Danes is omitted perhaps in deference to King Christian IV.

The Duncan of Holinshed is a soft, slack king, whose negligence in suppressing sedition was denounced by Macbeth. In the play he is elderly, gracious and saintly.

Macbeth felt that Duncan by making Malcolm Prince of Northumberland, and thereby heir to the throne, was unjustly setting aside his own legal right to succeed. Shakespeare suppresses this altogether.

For the wassailing of the two chamberlains and their subsequent murder by Macbeth, Shakespeare went to Holinshed's earlier account of the murder of King Duff by Macdonwald.

Banquo, according to Holinshed was one of Macbeth's accomplices in the murder. As he was the legendary ancestor of James I this is omitted, and Shakespeare gives him a speech of resounding integrity (II. iii, 123–5).

The play makes no mention of Macbeth's ten years of exemplary rule, nor of the building of Dunsinane castle by the thanes (except Macduff), nor Macbeth's siege of Macduff's castle, nor Macbeth's flight from Dunsinane.

II

SHAKESPEARE'S THEATRE

ALTHOUGH the evidence for the design of Elizabethan theatres is incomplete and conflicting, and although there were certainly differences of construction and arrangement, the following account, it is hoped, will give a reasonable outline.

The first public theatres in London were built during Shakespeare's lifetime, but they embodied in their design and construction the experience and practice of the medieval and Tudor play productions in inn yards, booth stages, and pageant wagons.

From square, circular or hexagonal theatre walls tiered with galleries for spectators, the Elizabethan stage jutted out over six feet above ground level and occupied about half the floor space where the spectators could stand on three sides of it. The stage of the Fortune theatre was 43 feet x 27 feet and the floor area in which it stood was 55 feet x 55 feet. At the back of the stage the lowest tier of spectators' galleries gave place to a curtained recess or inner stage, a study or discovery space, used for interior scenes. Another view is that there was no recess, but a curtained space under a canopy in front of the rear wall of the stage. On either side were dressing rooms from which entrance doors opened on to the stage. The first gallery behind the stage was used for scenes in the play; a second floor gallery or room was used by musicians. Above the balcony and covering the rear portion of the stage was a canopy or roof painted blue and adorned with stars sometimes supported by pillars from the stage. There were trap-doors in the stage and frequently a low rail around it.

The pillars, canopy, railings and back stage were painted and adorned. If a tragedy was to be performed, the stage was hung with black, but there was no set staging in the modern fashion.

There were stage properties usually of the kind that could be easily pushed on and off the stage. Records of the time mention a mossy bank, a wall, a bed, trees, arbours, thrones, tents, rock, tomb, hell-mouth, a cauldron; on the other hand tents, pavilions, and mansions may have been permanent 'sets' in some historical plays. These structures varied in size for a small one may have sufficed for the tomb in *Romeo and Juliet*,

MODEL OF AN ELIZABETHAN THEATRE
by Richard Southern

but the tent representing the Queen's chamber in Peele's *Edward I* contained six adults and a bed, as Armstrong pointed out. On the whole properties were limited to essentials although the popularity of the private masques with their painted canvas sets encouraged increasing elaboration of scenery and spectacle during the reign of James I.

There was no limitation to the display of rich and gorgeous costumes in the current fashion of the day. The more magnificent and splendid the better; indeed the costumes must have been the most expensive item in the requirements of the company. An occasional attempt was made at period costume, but normally plays were produced in Elizabethan garments without any suspicion of the oddness that strikes us when we read of Cæsar entering 'in his nightshirt' or Cleopatra calling on Charmian to cut the lace of what we may call her corsets. High rank was marked by magnificence of dress, a trade or calling by functional clothes. Feste, the clown, would wear the traditional fool's coat or petticoat of motley, a coarse cloth of mixed yellow and green. The coat was buttoned from the neck to the girdle from which hung a wooden dagger. Its skirts voluminous with capacious pockets in which Feste might 'impetticoat' any 'gratillity'. Ghosts, who appear in a number of plays, wore a kind of leathern smock. Oberon and magicians such as Prospero wore, in the delightful phrase and spelling of the records, 'a robe for to goo invisibell'.

The actors formed companies under the patronage of noblemen for protection against a civic law condemning them as 'rogues, vagabonds and sturdy beggars' to severe punishment. They were the servants of their patron and wore his livery. The company was a co-operative society, its members jointly owned the property and shared the profits; thus Shakespeare's plays were not his to use as he liked, they belonged to his company, the Lord Chamberlain's Men. This company, honoured by James I when it became the King's Men, was the most successful company of the period. It had a number of distinguished actors, it achieved more Court performances then any other company, and it performed in the best London theatre, the Globe, until it was burnt down during a performance of *Henry VIII* in 1613. Women were not allowed on the public stage, although they performed in masques and theatricals in private houses. Boys, therefore, were apprenticed to the leading actors and took the female parts.

The audience in the public theatres was drawn from all classes. There were courtiers and inns of court men who appreciated intricate word play, mythological allusions and the technique of sword play; there were the 'groundlings' who liked jigs, horse-play and flamboyance of speech and spectacle; and there were the citizens who appreciated the romantic stories, the high eloquence of patriotic plays and moral sentiments. A successful play would have something for all. Sometimes gallants would sit on a stool on the stage and behave rather like the courtiers in *A Midsummer Night's Dream*, V. i, or *Love's Labour's Lost*, V. ii. The 'groundlings' too were likely to be troublesome and noisy. They could buy bottled-beer, oranges and nuts for their comfort; but it is noted to their credit that when Falstaff appeared on the stage, so popular was he that they stopped cracking nuts! They applauded a well delivered speech; they hissed a boring play; they even rioted and severely damaged one theatre. Shakespeare's plays however were popular among all classes: at Court they

> did so take Eliza and our James,

and elsewhere in the public theatre they outshone the plays of other dramatists. Any play of his was assured of a 'full house'. An ardent theatre-goer of the day praising Shakespeare's plays above those of other dramatists wrote:

> When let but Falstaff come,
> Hal, Poins, the rest, you scarce shall have a room,
> All is so pester'd; let but Beatrice
> And Benedick be seen, lo in a trice
> The cockpit, galleries, boxes, all are full
> To hear Malvolio, that cross-garter'd gull.

III

THE HECATE SCENES

THE Hecate scenes, III. v; IV. i, 39–43, 125–32, are generally regarded as the work of another writer, added perhaps after Dr. Forman saw the play in 1611, for he makes no mention of Hecate. Although the words 'Come away come away' and 'Black spirits' are thought to belong to two songs in Middleton's play *The Witch* (1610?), it is not now considered that Middleton was the interpolator. The explanations put forward to account for the insertion of these scenes are singularly unconvincing. Thus the Arden editor believes that the Hecate passages were all written to 'explain and introduce the two songs and the dance which had been interpolated from *The Witch*'.

This assumption of interpolation is based on the two songs, signs of textual confusion, the substance and phrasing of Hecate's speeches, and her iambic tetrameter verse. The Folio entry notice 'Enter Hecate, and the three other Witches' (IV. i, 39) suggests that whoever inserted it did not realize that the Weird Sisters were already on the stage. There was no exit notice for Hecate. It is also suggested that the insertion of the Hecate scene necessitated interchanging of the present scenes III. vi and IV. i thereby causing the chronological disorder of the announcements of Macduff's flight to England. Hecate's scolding of the witches, her 'prettiness of lyrical fancy', and the incongruity of III. v, 10–13 and IV. i, 39–40 with the other witch scenes suggest a naive, trivial and alien conception out of harmony with the rest of the play. Hecate speaks entirely in iambic octosyllabic couplets, whereas Shakespeare elsewhere employs trochaic metre in songs or similar verse passages.

Flatter makes a number of points in defence of the genuineness of the Hecate scenes. The entry of Hecate is carefully prepared in typical Shakespearian fashion by references beforehand (II. i, 51–2; III. ii, 41). She has the function in III, v of giving advance information necessary to the understanding of the cauldron scene. The announcement of plans for their next meeting comes more effectively from Hecate than it would do from the Witches. The last part of her speech foreshadows Macbeth's psychological development, and raises tension and suspense as the audience sees that the forces of evil are gathering against him. The entry notice 'Enter Hecate, and the three other Witches' does not imply six witches altogether. Similar notices containing the names of characters already on the stage occur elsewhere (*Romeo and Juliet* V. ii; *Antony and Cleopatra*, V. ii; *A Midsummer Night's Dream*, III. i; IV. i, etc). The words 'Come away, come away' and 'Black spirits' were intended to be repeated ad lib until Hecate was out of sight. Shakespeare normally uses 'etc' to indicate the repetition of a refrain. There is no example elsewhere in Shakespeare's plays where a passage of dialogue and aria is so omitted. Hecate uses iambic metre but so do the Witches, I. i, 2, 8; I. iii, 4–10, 18, 30–1, 36; IV. i, 69, 75–6, 125–132, and the Apparitions, IV. i, 71 ff.

Two further notes may be contributed to the debate. Hecate in *Macbeth* is similar in function and shadowiness to the Devil in such morality plays as *Lusty Juventus*, *Like Will to Like*, *Susanna*, and *All for Money*. There his appearance is confined to one, or at most two, scenes in which he urges the Vice to carry out his plans to ruin mankind. He never comes into contact with human characters, and is a colourless, insipid creature of evil whose function is to make clear to the audience the evil intended against the central character. Hecate has more dignity than the Devil, but otherwise the resemblance is close.

The morality theme of the play with its antithesis of good and evil is precisely and traditionally patterned by the balanced opposition of the Pit of Acheron and the Court of Edward the Confessor, the House of the Ruler of Hell and the House of Divine Kingship. The two protagonists Macbeth and Macduff both journey each to the House whence he hopes to receive strength before the final encounter.

Shakespeare's Works

The year of composition of only a few of Shakespeare's plays can be determined with certainty. The following list is based on current scholarly opinion.

The plays marked with an asterisk were not included in the First Folio edition of Shakespeare's plays (1623) which was prepared by Heminge and Condell, Shakespeare's fellow actors. Shakespeare's part in them has been much debated.

1590–1 2 Henry VI, 3 Henry VI.

1591–2 1 Henry VI.

1592–3 Richard III, Comedy of Errors.

1593–4 Titus Andronicus, Taming of the Shrew, Sir Thomas More★ (Part authorship. Four manuscript pages presumed to be in Shakespeare's hand).

1594–5 Two Gentlemen of Verona, Love's Labour's Lost, Romeo and Juliet, Edward III★ (Part authorship).

1595–6 Richard II, A Midsummer Night's Dream.

1596–7 King John, Merchant of Venice, Love's Labour Won (Not extant. Before 1598).

1597–8 1 Henry IV, 2 Henry IV, The Merry Wives of Windsor.

1598–9 Much Ado About Nothing, Henry V.

1599–1600 Julius Caesar, As You Like It.

1600–1 Hamlet, Twelfth Night.

1601–2 Troilus and Cressida.

1602–3 All's Well that Ends Well.

Moved to S   heatre
which he and his company had recently erected.

1602 Extensive purchases of property and land in Stratford.

1602–4 Lodged with Mountjoy, a Huguenot refugee and a maker of headdresses, in Cripplegate, London. Helped to arrange a marriage between Mary Mountjoy and Stephen Belott, her father's apprentice.

1603 His company became the King's Majesty's Players under royal patronage.

1607 His daughter Susanna married Dr John Hall.

1608 Birth of Shakespeare's grand-daughter Elizabeth Hall.

1610 Shakespeare possibly returned to live in Stratford.

1613 Purchase of the Gatehouse in Blackfriars. Burning of the Globe Theatre during the premiere of *Henry VIII*.

1616 Marriage of his daughter Judith to Thomas Quiney in Lent for which they were excommunicated.

25 March, 1616 Shakespeare altered the draft of his will presumably to give Judith more security in view of her husband's unreliability and his pre-marital misconduct with another woman. His will also revealed his strong attachment to his Stratford friends, and above all his desire to arrange for the establishment of his descendants.

23 April, 1616 Death of Shakespeare.

1623 Publication of the First Folio edition of Shakespeare's plays collected by his fellow actors Heminge and Condell to preserve 'the memory of so worthy a friend'.